"By the time you reach the end of the book . . . you will have triggered many memories and given much thought to the overall shape of your spiritual life.

"For me, the writing of *ARC OF THE ARROW* has brought together many strands of experience. I have spent most of my three decades of professional life writing the stories of historical figures, attempting to find, through research in contemporary records, the inner drives and motivations that made these people from the past who they were. In every case I have encountered, beyond the personality, character and historical circumstances of my subject, another dimension: the dimension of spirit. In interpreting the lives of my subjects—and there is no biographical writing that is worth anything that does not have an interpretive element—I found I had to come to terms with the unfolding of their spiritual selves.

"I hope that whatever is of value in the pages that follow transcends religious categories and will be of use to all spiritual seekers, especially those curious to discern and pursue the working of the spirit in their lives."

—Carolly Erickson, from the introduction

Other Books by Carolly Erickson

The Records of Medieval Europe
Civilization and Society in the West
The Medieval Vision
Bloody Mary
Great Harry
The First Elizabeth
Mistress Anne
Our Tempestuous Day: A History of Regency England
Bonnie Prince Charlie
To the Scaffold: The Life of Marie Antoinette
Great Catherine
Her Little Majesty: The Life of Queen Victoria
Season of the Swan: The Life of Josephine
    (Forthcoming from St. Martin's Press)

ARC
OF THE
ARROW

WRITING YOUR SPIRITUAL AUTOBIOGRAPHY

Carolly Erickson

POCKET BOOKS
New York   London   Toronto   Sydney   Tokyo   Singapore

An *Original* Publication of POCKET BOOKS

 POCKET BOOKS, a division of Simon & Schuster Inc.
1230 Avenue of the Americas, New York, NY 10020

ISBN: 0-671-01745-4

First Pocket Books trade paperback printing April 1998

10 9 8 7 6 5 4 3 2 1

POCKET and colophon are registered trademarks of Simon & Schuster Inc.

Cover design by Jeanne M. Lee
Cover illustration by John Nickle

Printed in the U.S.A.

To the memory of my beloved grandmother
Edna M. Kiger
and the Glendale Truth Center

My dark and cloudy words they do but hold
The truth, as cabinets enclose the gold.

—John Bunyan, *The Pilgrim's Progress*

The arrow flies, loosed from what unseen bow
Toward what unseen goal I cannot discern.
The arrow flies, trackless, silent, sure of
Purpose, its arc my life. My soul the
Arrow, my journey its path, my heart borne
Along its arc. The arc complete,
The arrow falls to earth. The archer bends
His bow anew.

CONTENTS

INTRODUCTION

As the millennium approaches, we are increasingly preoccupied with the things of the spirit. Whether or not we are members of a religious congregation, or are engaged in a regular religious practice, we are attending more and more to the business of looking inward, seeking to understand that part of ourselves that transcends flesh and blood.

More and more, we are coming to realize that, along with our bodies, our intellects and our hearts, we possess spiritual selves, resilient when confronted with tragedy or hardship, resistant when menaced by oppression, courageous amid disaster.

From birth to death, while our bodies drive themselves to labor and lend themselves to pleasure, while our minds learn, scheme and plan, our hearts experience love and joy, pain and loss, our spiritual selves too are alive and at work, though the course and end of that work may not always be apparent.

Christian theology teaches that there is an immaterial part of each man and woman called the soul, an eternal essence that indwells the body and survives after the body dies. In the theological concept of the Trinity, the divine is described as God the father, God the son and God the holy spirit, the latter an invisible comforter who works within each believer, as near as breath, to inspire and draw him or her inward toward their spiritual core.

Many religious traditions have similar beliefs. But one need not subscribe to a particular doctrine, or believe in an afterlife or in reincarnation, to observe that there is an indefinable, ineffable part of us that operates powerfully to buoy us up and carry us lifeward and God-ward. It is our spirit that heals when medicine fails and purely physical resources run out. Similarly, it is the ebbing of the spirit that often signals the onset of death—"giving up the ghost," to use an old expression.

The spirit may be envisioned as the irreducible essence of our selves, adamantine and splendorous, stronger than our strongest willpower, sensed yet incomprehensible.

A useful working definition of the spirit is that it is that force within us that links us to whatever higher power we acknowledge—that power we call by the name of the divine.

One of the best ways to explore the working of that power in your life is to write your life story—not an account of your entire life, but the story of your spiritual self, your spiritual autobiography. The purpose of this book is to help you carry out that effort, by introducing you to several ways others have written the stories of their spiritual lives in the past, and then by guiding you to bring together the materials that will form the basis of your own storytelling.

Along the way, exercises are provided to get you started in your writing—and to stimulate your thinking about your past experience and about the nature of your spiritual life. The exercises call for brief written responses at first, then lead you into more complex writing efforts. By the time you reach the end of the book, if you carry out the exercises faithfully, you will be well on the way to producing your autobiography, and in the process you will have triggered many memories and given much thought to the overall shape of your spiritual life.

For me, the writing of *Arc of the Arrow* has brought together many strands of experience. I have spent most of my three decades of professional life writing the life stories of historical figures, attempting to find, through research in contemporary records, the inner drives and motivations that made these people from the past who they were. In every case I have encountered, beyond the personality, character and historical circumstances of my subject, another dimension: the dimension of spirit. In interpreting the lives of my subjects—and there is no biographical writing that is worth anything that does not have an interpretive element—I found I had to come to terms with the unfolding of their spiritual selves.

I am aware that this interest of mine is rooted in my own spiritual past, as the daughter and granddaughter of spiritual teachers who ran a storefront church of no definable denomination and as the survivor of a somewhat bizarre childhood in which I spent time among Mormons, Presbyterians, and (more briefly) Episcopalians and Catholics. I even played the organ in a funeral chapel on occasion, when my mother was called in on short notice to conduct a funeral service for someone she had never met.

It is safe to say that I was steeped in the spiritual, even entangled in it; I emerged from this immersion with a lifelong fascination with the psychology of religion and—more fortunately—a deepgoing if erratic faith.

In recent years I have had the opportunity to explore an interest in spiritual autobiography, an interest that led indirectly to the writing of this book.

Although I am writing as a Protestant Christian,

and make no claim to know any other faith system well, I hope that whatever is of value in the pages that follow transcends religious categories and will be of use to all spiritual seekers, especially those curious to discern and pursue the working of the spirit in their lives.

I

JOHN BUNYAN
AND THE WAY
OF THE PILGRIM

*M*ore than three hundred years ago John Bunyan, an English tinsmith who was also a wandering preacher, wrote a book that became an overnight success. It was called *The Pilgrim's Progress,* and it told the story of an anguished man struggling to find his way from the darkness of the world toward the light of salvation.

Because Bunyan wrote the story of his hero, whom he named Christian, in a vivid and page-turning style, and because his story contains many memorable characters and adventurous episodes, it has been read by generations of believers who see in it echoes of their own often laborious progress toward their ultimate goal.

The action of the story takes place in an imagined

landscape, which might be called the landscape of the psyche. It has hills and valleys, rivers and trees, like the material landscape of earth, but from the very beginning Bunyan leads us into an alternative world, a landscape of the religious imagination, where states of mind and attitudes and qualities of character have shapes and forms, some human, some inanimate.

To follow the arduous pilgrimage of Christian over this psychic terrain is to encounter, in outward form, many of the pitfalls and triumphs we encounter inwardly in the course of our lives. For this reason, *The Pilgrim's Progress* offers a fruitful paradigm for spiritual autobiography.

Bunyan's tale begins when Christian, who lives with his wife and four children in the City of Destruction, flees his home in search of eternal life. Clothed in rags, and bearing a heavy burden on his back, Christian meets Evangelist, who shows him the gate that leads to the path he must follow—the straight and narrow path whose end is the Celestial City. But Christian no sooner enters the path than he is enmired in a bog, the Swamp of Dejection, where he loses heart and founders. He is tempted to return home, but help arrives, and, with his understanding strengthened, Christian enters a highway called Salvation that leads to the cross.

At the cross his burden falls from his back, and he cries aloud for joy. Now sealed with the mark of

Christ, the pilgrim resumes his journey, shrugging off the bad advice of fellow journeyers who urge him to take an easier path than the one he is on. But soon he meets with another threat: two fierce lions who rise up to menace his progress. Undaunted, Christian successfully passes this trial of faith, and enjoys a respite in the Chamber of Peace in the Palace Beautiful, where he glimpses Immanuel's Land, an arcadian country, abundantly watered with springs and fountains and planted in vineyards and orchards that offers, on the far horizon, a vista of the Celestial City.

The vista is tantalizingly brief, for soon Christian finds himself in the Valley of Humiliation, facing a winged monster Apollyon (in Revelation 9:11, Apollyon is the angel of the bottomless pit, and king of the swarm of locusts sent to torment the unsaved), who commands him to leave his quest for the Celestial City and return to the City of Destruction, on pain of death. For many hours Christian endures the flaming darts and blows of the monster, wounded repeatedly, disarmed, and weakening until he feels he is at the point of death. At the last possible moment, summoning all his remaining strength, Christian manages to regain his sword and stab Apollyon, who is vanquished and flies off.

Hardly has he passed through this dread challenge than Christian is faced with a worse one. He enters the Valley of the Shadow of Death, made almost as black as night by overhanging clouds of confusion. Howling spirits gather around him and frighten him as he begins to walk along an extremely narrow ledge between a deep ditch and a quagmire, fearing, as he takes each successive step, that he will miss his footing in the dark. In his terror Christian thinks yet again of turning back and retracing his steps toward the City of Destruction, especially when he sees, in the side of a hill, the flaming, smoke-filled entrance to hell.

Surrounded by tormenting fiends, in constant apprehension of death, with only prayer and his pilgrim faith to sustain him, Christian plods on through the endless dark valley, his wits so confounded at times that he cannot even recognize the sound of his own voice. Traps, snares and pitfalls menace his every step, and he is reminded of his own mortal danger by the sight of the bones, ashes, and mangled bodies of other pilgrims who had preceded him and who had fallen prey to the manifold hazards in the valley.

Finally Christian's path leads him out of the valley, and he continues his journey with a companion, Faithful, and together they come to the town of Vanity, the site of a great fair or marketplace. The temptations of Vanity Fair are very great, for every worldly prize is for sale there: not only houses, estates, and chests of treasure but high offices, power and influence, even entire kingdoms, plus the means to assuage every sensual desire. The chief lord of the fair, the devil Beelzebub, presides over this festival of worldly offerings, providing entertainment for all and turning a blind eye to the lawbreaking, theft, even murder that goes on in his domain.

Christian and Faithful resist the allure of Beelzebub's fair, averting their eyes from the glittering offerings and buying nothing. They are despised for their attitude, seized and beaten repeatedly, and thrown into an iron cage. Brought to trial before Judge Hategood for their contempt of all that the world has to offer, the two pilgrims are condemned to execution, and Faithful dies at the hands of his persecutors. Christian, however, manages to escape, and finds another companion, Hopeful, with whom he rests in a plain called Ease near the river of the water of life.

Resuming their journey, the pilgrims take a wrong turning, and eventually come to Doubting Castle, presided over by the giant Despair. Now comes Christian's severest trial, for the giant beats both men unmercifully and throws them into his stinking, disease-ridden dungeon and leaves them there, without food or water, for four endlessly long days. Their hearts sink, and Despair assails them continuously, trying to convince them to kill themselves, as there is no hope of their ever being restored to health or liberty.

To outbrave external danger is one thing, but to fight off the gnawing, uncontrollable inward conviction of hopelessness is quite another. Christian, inclined to choose the grave over the dungeon, seriously considers taking Despair's advice. But Hopeful pulls him back from the brink, reminding him of how far he has come and what valor he has shown in averting many dangers; can he not summon the strength of will and faith to resist the urge to do away with himself?

A prolonged prayer vigil brings into Christian's tortured mind the memory of a key with which he has been presented—the key called Promise. With it he unlocks the door of Despair's dungeon and walks free.

Passing safely through the Enchanted Ground, a region where they become drowsy and are tempted to enter an eternal sleep, Christian and Faithful arrive in Beulah Land, where the sun shines day and night and where the Shining Ones, bright messengers of God, walk abroad. From Beulah Land they can see the Celestial City, built of pearls and precious stones and gleaming with such brightness that they cannot bear to look at it directly.

But before they can reach the gates of the city, one more trial awaits. A deep river, the river of Death, divides the pilgrims from their destination. They are told that the depth of the river will be according to the firmness of their faith. At this ultimate terror, the terror of drowning and losing all that he has fought so hard to gain, Christian once again falters. He enters the river, but soon cries out that he is sinking. Hopeful urges Christian on, and holds his head above the surging waters, but Christian has difficulty believing that he can overcome death, and his senses fail him.

"Be of good cheer," says Hopeful. "Jesus Christ maketh thee whole." Hopeful's words penetrate the veil that has fallen over Christian's awareness, and he gropes once again to see the face of Christ. The image clarifies, and Christian begins to find his footing.

Now Christian and Hopeful ascend the hill that leads to the great golden gate of the Celestial City. With a crowd of heavenly greeters to accompany them, trumpets sounding and bells ringing in joyful cacophany, their faces shining, they arrive at last at their destination, and enter, as Bunyan writes, "into the joy of the Lord."

THE PILGRIM MENTALITY

Bunyan's story is more complex than this brief retelling of it, but I have included the essentials. It is inviting and somehow satisfying to view one's spiritual life as a journey, with birth (or perhaps a childhood baptism or confession of faith or other religious event) marking the beginning of the road or path and death marking the ultimate arrival.

We may experience our spiritual lives as a series of episodes, or encounters with unforeseen events or conditions, forming no consistent pattern—like a meandering river that winds from one bend to the next. In tracing this life course, we might follow Bunyan and give names to the prominent features in our psychic landscape: Mount Martyrdom, the Arbor of Lust, the Vale of Success, the Cave of Wealth, the Thicket of Deceit, the Wasteland of Divorce.

The hills, fruitful meadows, quagmires, dark shadowed valleys and overflowing rivers of our experience may seem to lead us onward toward a worthy goal, or they may cause us to double back on ourselves, to regress, or even to return to our starting point—or to our own personal City of Destruction where psychic dangers lurk.

But just as in Bunyan's spiritual map, we will probably recall seasons of ease, peace and renewal, and important spiritual companions who gave us encouragement and showed us the way when we were lost.

The pilgrim journey is sharply focused; it is a quest, in search of an ultimate prize. Our spiritual lives are rarely so one-pointed. In thinking about your journey, you may identify long stretches of time spent in Pastures of Dullness or Plains of Inattention when your spiritual awareness dimmed. Or you may have tarried in temples of agnosticism or fortresses of atheism, or built shrines of your own to deities (persons, ideologies, career goals) that, for a time, seemed to promise meaningful rewards but which you ultimately abandoned.

The way of the pilgrim is to be in this world but not of it—to be always restless in the midst of earthly life and longing for that higher, purer, transcendent realm that lies in the far distance, at the end of the journey. Thus the mentality of the pilgrim is that of a rootless wanderer, a sojourner in a foreign place (for all places are foreign to one who cannot be at home until he completes his quest). It is not a comfortable frame of mind, or an easy one; the pilgrim looks out on the world with a wistful gaze, and a watchful one, for he expects dangers and difficulties.

For the pilgrim, life is a struggle against snares and temptations, dangers and challenges. To be sure, there are oases of refreshment and rest amid the strife, but the struggle is neverending and constant vigilance is essential. If the tale of Christian's journey appeals to you, it may be because, on some deep level, you are always comparing everyday life with its flaws to an ideal or utopia, whether spiritual or secular, where perfection reigns. You may look on the world as a hostile place, or at least a dangerous one. Or you may simply be gifted with a vision of betterment, an unquenchable hope for humanity that finds spiritual expression in the ability to look beyond the mundane and in the prayerful or meditative contemplation of your own understanding of the Celestial City.

EXERCISES:
THE WAY OF THE PILGRIM AND
YOUR SPIRITUAL STORY

1. Using as large a sheet of paper as you have available (art paper two feet square is ideal), draw a map of your spiritual journey, naming important landmarks along the way. Do this in any way that feels appropriate to you—as a landscape with mountains and valleys, rivers and lakes, as a "flow chart" with arrows and boxes, as a series of pictures or images, as a blueprint. Let your map reflect who you are and the lens through which you view the world.

Although your journey is not yet complete, indicate, perhaps with a dotted line, where you think it is leading and what your ultimate destination will be.

2. Choose three episodes from the story of Christian the pilgrim (for example, the fight with the winged monster Apollyon, the encounter with the giant Despair, and the temptations of Vanity Fair) and relate them to occasions in your spiritual life.

....

....

....

....

....

....

....

....

....

....

....

....

....

....

....

....

....

....

....

....

3. Who in your life has played the role of Faithful? Hopeful? Evangelist?

2

Augustine of Hippo and the Way of the Intellectual Seeker

In *The Pilgrim's Progress* we followed in the footsteps of a literary character, Christian the pilgrim, an Everyman (or Everywoman) whose journey through life in many ways resembled our own. In the *Confessions* of Augustine we meet, not a literary character, but a real person, whose spiritual life was a prolonged quest to understand, and finally to accept, the Christian revelation.

Augustine, who was born in a small town in what is now Algeria in North Africa in the middle of the fourth century, grew up in an unsettled, often chaotic era. Like many of his contemporaries, he felt with disturbing certainty that his world was crumbling.

The Roman Empire still ruled the Mediterranean

world, but the area it controlled was shrinking. Conflict with Germanic tribes in the borderlands meant ongoing loss of territory, while cultural conflict between the traditional pagan religion of Rome and a host of newer faiths, among them Christianity, led to confusion and debate in the realm of ideas.

Into this ferment stepped the gifted young Augustine, son of a pagan father and a Christian mother, Monica, whose cherishing love and prayerful guidance was a strong and formative influence.

Augustine tells us in his *Confessions* that one of his earliest memories was of praying to God that he might not be beaten at school. As sensitive as he was intelligent, he was afraid to be punished—and punishment was likely, because despite his superior abilities as a writer and orator, the youthful Augustine hated his Greek lessons and disobeyed both his masters and his parents.

In Augustine's boyhood it was not usual for Christians to be baptized until the end of their lives, so although Monica raised Augustine as a believer, he was not a full participant in the local church, nor had he a strong or deep attachment to the Christian faith. Living as he did surrounded by many competing religions, including some that were of more recent origin and more vital than Christianity, he was distracted by the smorgasbord of faiths and pulled increasingly toward a position of skepticism.

At the same time, he writes in his *Confessions,* he

was, at about the age of fifteen, led into petty theft
by his boyhood companions and, soon afterward, assaulted by "the madness of lust" so that he sought
out prostitutes and even seduced married women.
Augustine's father was inclined to view his son's
sexual adventurism tolerantly—after all, it meant
that one day there would be grandchildren—but
Monica fretted and prayed and gave her son un-
heeded advice.

Augustine's education in worldliness continued as
his training in rhetoric, the art of elegant and per-
suasive public speaking, advanced. The older he got,
and the more outstanding he became as an orator
(he was soon the envy of all his fellow students in
the city of Carthage), the more boldly he plunged
into what he called the "cauldron of unholy loves,"
walking "the streets of Babylon" with unworthy
companions and carousing with them and making
mischief.

In a famous passage in the *Confessions*, he de-
scribes how with his gang of local toughs he invaded
an orchard and stripped a pear tree bare (the pear
was a symbol of lust, as he well knew), flinging the
fruit to the hogs. Recalling this wanton act years
later, as a mature adult, Augustine was mortified; it
was not that the fruit was tempting, merely that the
act of stealing it was forbidden, that made him and
his companions do what they did.

At Carthage, Augustine read Cicero's *Hortensius*

and felt the first stirrings of a longing that would never leave him—the longing to attain wisdom. He sought it in the Christian Scriptures, but his education in the Latin classics had made him scornful of the relatively plain language and unadorned style of the biblical texts, and he rejected texts and teachings alike.

Instead, he began to study the teachings of the Manicheans, a numerous and popular religious sect that recognized and worshiped two deities, God and Satan; according to the Manicheans, God ruled in the realm of light and the spirit, while Satan ruled over the realm of darkness and material things. While not everything about Manichean beliefs was clear to Augustine, he embraced them because they satisfied most of his need to understand the world in a way that was both systematic and profound, and for ten years he was a faithful member of the Manichean community and brought others into it as well.

Meanwhile he made the transition from student to teacher of rhetoric, precociously brilliant, much admired by his circle of devoted friends, and with a more settled personal life. He did not marry, but lived with a woman ("one whom I had found out in a wayward passion," he says) as his concubine. With her he had a son whose name, Adeodatus, means "God's gift."

Thus Augustine arrived at the exalted age of

thirty—a riper age in the fourth century than now, because of the shorter life expectancy then prevailing. He had great gifts: a powerful mind, an able tongue, a nimble wit, strong emotions and a passionate if divided heart. He had attained much. He had great skill as a rhetorician, he had renown, and he had a close bond with his concubine and son.

Inwardly, however, as he writes in his *Confessions*, Augustine was estranged from himself. "I became a great riddle to myself," he said. "I became to myself a barren land." He wrote of his "shattered and bleeding soul," a soul unsatisfied, like his active and searching mind. Restless, always seeking inner peace through a deeper understanding of his place in the order of things—an order whose outlines seemed to grow less and less clear with each passing year—Augustine was persuaded to go to Rome where greater fame awaited him.

His mother urged him not to go, fearing that his sense of inner estrangement would only increase in the citadel of paganism, the imperial capital. Deceiving her about his plans, Augustine left hurriedly for Rome—only to discover, once he had begun to establish himself there as a teacher of rhetoric, that the students had a habit of cheating teachers of their fees, and that he was no more content than he had been in Carthage.

He had become increasingly disillusioned with Manicheism, and began investigating the writings of the Neoplatonists. In accepting the Neoplatonist teaching that all things, spiritual and material, were created from a divine source called the One, Augustine moved closer to Christianity, yet he still resisted accepting the divinity of Jesus and the redemptive message of the cross. His mind, that fierce taskmaster, drove him to endless analysis and weighing of philosophical issues, especially the question of where evil came from.

Increasingly rootless in his personal life—though it broke his heart to do so, he gave up the concubine he loved and sought to marry a girl from a wealthy family of high status, though this attempt came to nothing—he churned restlessly in his professional life as well, moving to Milan in search of still greater fame and official honors.

Now all was confusion. Augustine was approaching thirty-three, gnawed by doubts and ambivalent about his future. Part of him wanted to try to become a high official in the imperial court, but this meant attaching his fate to that of the crumbling Empire. Another part of him longed to retire to the countryside to live communally with a group of like-minded friends, studying philosophy and living a contemplative life, but this meant giving up all that he had worked toward from the age of seventeen.

Where did certainty lie, he asked himself again and again. What philosophical or religious anchor was there to ground him, amid the storm and wrack of an age of turmoil and transformation?

The answer was slow in coming, but Augustine began to perceive it, not in reading or studying or logical thought, but in the person of the Bishop of Milan, Ambrose, spiritual father to the community of Milanese Christians and therefore to Augustine himself. The bishop was a highly educated former government official who spoke with the eloquence of Cicero, thus exemplifying the best that the civilization of Rome had to offer, yet he chose to dedicate his eloquence and intellect to the service of the church.

Moved greatly by Ambrose's example, Augustine geared himself up to confront his inner demons once and for all. One afternoon he had a vision of himself as "crooked and defiled, bespotted and ulcerous." He could not argue himself out of this conviction of shame and self-revulsion; indeed all argument seemed useless, and wearily he laid his intellect aside.

Deeply troubled, "pressed in his inward parts" by God, lashed by fear and shame, yet no longer demanding to understand, merely seeking to surrender to "belief in the way of the Lord," whatever that might mean, Augustine sat down under a fig tree in a garden and began to cry.

He was aware of a child's voice in the distance saying "Take up and read, take up and read." In response to this mysterious voice, he began to read the words of St. Paul, his eye alighting by chance on the verse, "Not in rioting or drunkenness, not in chambering and wantonness, not in strife and envying, but put ye on the Lord Jesus Christ, and make not provision for the flesh, in concupiscence." All at once, he writes, his confusion was dispelled, his heart was lightened and filled with serenity, and all the darkness of doubt vanished. In one remarkable moment, he had turned from his former life, and had been made whole again.

Soon after Augustine's dramatic conversion he was baptized by Ambrose, and he laid aside his teaching in order to embrace a retired life of study and devotion. The narrative of Augustine's autobiography in the *Confessions* ends with his conversion, but he lived on for many more years, eventually becoming Bishop of Hippo in North Africa and preaching, ministering and writing voluminously. No Christian writer for the next eight hundred years had greater influence on Western thought and learning.

THE MENTALITY OF THE INTELLECTUAL SEEKER

The story of Augustine's long and frustrating search for truth, culminating in his conversion, offers a compelling model of spiritual autobiography. His neverending seeking for answers to the time-honored questions—is there more to life than the material world that we perceive with our senses, where do I fit in the grand scheme of things, what is the meaning of my life, why do tragedy, loss and pain have to happen, and if God exists, why does he allow these evils into his creation?—led him to discover ever more satisfying levels of understanding, in an upward spiral of discernment.

Thus whereas Christian the pilgrim plunged bravely on, uphill and down, holding fast to his vision of the Celestial City, Augustine sought to rise above the terrestrial plane, into a realm of abstraction and philosophical inquiry, having no clear end in sight but peace of mind and a state of perfect explanation.

But there is much more to the *Confessions* than philosophical inquiry. For if his mind was constantly restless and active, Augustine was also driven by his heart. His candor, his longing and passion, his admission of his heartrending anguish fairly burn off the page, and his autobiography contains some of the most eloquent descriptions of inner feeling ever written.

Augustine was fortunate in that, ultimately, he found his answer, his moment of truth, in his conversion experience. But it was not until he had set his mind aside and surrendered to the guidance he found elsewhere, in the depths of his spirit, that the light dawned and peace descended.

We may experience our spiritual lives as a quest for understanding, with greater and greater comprehension dawning as we reach each new turn of the gyre. For many people, acquiring the skills of critical thinking in college marks one turning; for others, reading an especially well-reasoned book or taking a course of study later in life, or puzzling out a knotty personal or professional problem bring about an advancement up the spiral of discernment.

Encounters with alternate belief systems—or even, as in Augustine's case, conversion from one religion or philosophical system to another—can take one to a different level of clarity about God and the reality that lies behind appearances.

We may or may not feel a kinship with Augustine's restlessness and anxiety, his loathing of self and deep dissatisfaction with his worldly success. But many of us will find his conversion experience familiar, that unique moment when, pressed by God and longing for relief from the stresses of life, we encounter, in hearing a Bible passage or in prayer or in some unexpected juncture of spirit, heart and will the sudden dawning of that certainty and serenity that turns us to God and makes us whole.

There is a purity and nobility about the way of the intellectual seeker. It is as if he or she has cast off the dross of everyday life in order to pursue only the essentials, to drive with full force of mind toward what is primal at its core. Insight, an instinct for the jugular, incisiveness and an ability to grasp and analyze complex ideas and to make unexpected connections are often the rewards of a well-trained and active mind, and these are rare treasures to be cherished.

But the way of the intellect is often strewn with thorns. Perhaps by definition, those who orient themselves toward the world primarily through their minds have difficulty, as Augustine did, in putting those minds aside. Greedy for ideas, hungry for mental food to ruminate on, the mind insists on occupying center stage—indeed there is a temptation to substitute our minds for God as arbiters of truth.

For the mentality of the intellectual seeker may, at times, be destructive of faith. Our analytical minds may attempt to reduce all things, including the things of the spirit, to human-centered, finite experience; the idea of a God-centered, infinite creation then becomes uncongenial—or worse, it begins to seem unnecessary.

Furthermore, when our minds are our primary tools for searching out spiritual truth, we have a tendency to lose sight of our own limitations, and to presume that our minds are more competent than they really are. As Augustine wrote in another of his books, "By what understanding shall man comprehend God, when he comprehends not his very intellect, whereby he would fain comprehend him?"

In other words, we overvalue our understanding and undervalue those things that lie outside it. We tend to lose touch with those aspects of the divine that lie outside all understanding—the unsearchable, unfathomable, ineffable mystery of God.

If the way of the intellectual seeker seems to be your path, you may find in the *Confessions* of Augustine a paradigm for your own quest for discernment. Like Augustine, you may feel an ardent longing for understanding, a passion for discovering the truth, that may have led you onward to ever higher levels of discovery.

You may, following the guidance of your intellect, have decided at some point in your life to discard all spiritual things. You may have found yourself in a state of confusion at times, then passed on, with the aid of fresh areas of thought or learning, into greater clarity. Perhaps after years of following the dictates of the mind alone, you have begun to feel a yearning for a wider understanding of what is, and why it is, than the mind alone can provide.

You may have experienced a dramatic (or a quiet and gradual) conversion, or more than one. Or you may, like Augustine, resist for a long time embracing any religious or philosophical system because it does not provide all the answers you seek.

Some seekers never find their answers; they spend their entire lives looking, meanwhile remaining rootless, feeling the lack of a weighty anchor to ground them. The fortunate ones are able, as Augustine finally was able, to set aside the demands of their minds long enough to hear the small voice of the spirit asking them to receive what is always being offered—guidance, consolation, hope. They come to realize that, just as the mind climbs its upward spiral, so too the spirit buoys us upward toward the light of truth, where we rest, enlightened and refreshed, awaiting the unfolding of that which is to come.

EXERCISES:
The Way of the Intellectual Seeker and Your Spiritual Story

1. Can you recall a time in your past when you were looking for answers to basic questions about the meaning of life through reading and study? Did your search bring you spiritual rewards? Write a brief description of that experience.

....

....

....

....

....

....

....

....

....

....

....

....

....

....

2. Have you "tried out" various belief systems at one time or another? Do you expect to continue in the spiritual beliefs you now hold for the rest of your life?

....
....
....
....
....
....
....
....
....
....
....
....
....
....
....
....
....
....
....
....
....

3. Have you experienced the anguish of "becoming to yourself a barren land" as Augustine did? What brought you back from that wasteland of spiritual barrenness?

....

....

....

....

....

....

....

....

....

....

....

....

....

....

....

....

....

....

....

....

4. If you are a convert, write a brief account of your conversion, including what led you to surrender to God.

....

....

....

....

....

....

....

....

....

....

....

....

....

....

....

....

....

....

....

....

....

....

3

THE BOOK OF JOB
AND THE WAY
OF THE AFFLICTED

$\mathcal{S}$ome time between the seventh century and the second century before the birth of Christ, a masterful poet wrote a long poetic treatment of a central question of faith: Why must innocent people suffer, and if God exists, why does he allow that suffering to happen?

Rather than treat the subject in an abstract way, the writer told a story, centered on a memorable character, Job, from the land of Uz. Job's tribulations, and the dialogue to which they gave rise, provide a useful paradigm for spiritual autobiography.

When the narrative begins, Job, an exceedingly wealthy man blessed with seven sons and three daughters, is enjoying an exceptionally favored life. Not only is he, as the poet tells us, "the greatest of all the men of the east," but he is rich in the respect of his relatives and friends and the people of his community. For he does not hoard his riches, but goes out of his way to be a benefactor to his community, helping the poor, supporting widows and orphans, aggressively seeking out criminals and making restitution where injustice has been done. Job himself says that he is "eyes to the blind, and feet to the lame"; he takes particular pride in living a righteous life and because of this, people often come to him for advice, listen intently, and go away satisfied.

Job is not arrogant, according to the poet, but he cannot help but notice in what high regard he is held. When he walks through the streets, young men duck out of sight and old men stand up as a sign of respect. Even princes refrain from conversation and observe silence in Job's presence. It is as if everything he touches prospers—his fields, his loved ones, his neighbors and those who benefit from his generosity. Abundance follows him, because God is with him, and he walks by God's light.

Suddenly one day everything changes. A messenger rushes in to tell Job that a band of enemy Sabeans have swept in and stolen all his oxen and donkeys, killing his field servants. Hardly has the first messenger finished telling his news than a second arrives to say that all Job's seven thousand sheep have been killed by a mysterious "fire from heaven," and meantime all his camels too have been stolen and their keepers slain.

Deeply distressed, Job has no time to prepare himself for the much more devastating news that soon comes. His ten children, he learns, have gathered in the eldest son's house for a feast. While they are there, a terrible windstorm howls around the house, lifting it up by the corners so that it collapses on all those inside. Job's seven sons are killed (the biblical narrative does not tell us the fate of the daughters, but presumably they died too).

In a matter of minutes, nearly all that Job possesses is torn from his grasp—his children, his flocks and herds, most of his servants. He stands up, tears his clothes, and, taking a razor, shaves his head as a sign of mourning. He falls on his face in reverence, and makes his response to God—a response that is almost a reflex, in its deeply pious submissiveness.

"Naked came I out of my mother's womb, and naked shall I return thither," Job says. "The Lord gave, and the Lord hath taken away; blessed be the name of the Lord."

But Job's tribulations are not over. Boils break out over every part of his body, from the soles of his feet to the crown of his head. He cannot walk, lie down, or even sit down without pain. The agony of his grief-stricken thoughts is matched by the physical agony he must endure. Now he is truly as wretched as a man can be, and he takes up a shard of pottery and tries, without success, to scrape the boils away.

His wife, hardly a passive witness to all that has happened, cries out to Job from her own anguish, demanding that he "curse God, and die." But Job refuses. If we receive blessings and abundance from God, Job tells her, why should we not also receive misfortune?

Job's unswerving faith astounds everyone, especially three of his friends, Eliphaz, Bildad and Zophar, who come to see him and to mourn with him in his suffering. For seven days and nights Job and his three friends commune silently together, sitting on the ground and grieving.

Then, on the eighth day, Job pours forth his lament. The reflexive responses, the automatic blessing of God for good and bad alike, have now subsided. Job curses the day he was born, and wishes that his mother had aborted him. He longs for death, so great is his suffering. "My roarings are poured out like the waters," he says—but he still does not turn against God.

His friends are loyal but not empathetic. Eliphaz urges Job to keep in mind that trouble is a natural part of life and that God has promised to rescue us from every sort of tribulation. Bildad is skeptical; when Job asserts that his suffering is unjust, because he has lived an upright life following God's laws, Bildad contradicts him. If you were truly righteous, Bildad says, then God would remove your afflictions. Zophar goes even further, asserting that God was probably punishing Job less than he actually deserved—and reminds him that God's ways are unknowable.

Job listens to the rather shallow exhortations of his friends with increasing bad temper. If only they could understand just how deep and how piercing his grief is! Each day his anguish grows, for his physical torment makes it impossible for him to sleep, and even when, in his extreme exhaustion, he does manage to fall asleep for a few minutes, nightmares waken him again. His skin is broken and loathsome, stinking with pustules, he is "clothed with worms and clods of dust." Every moment seems to burden him with more pain, so that he longs for death.

What makes Job's suffering especially keen is that he knows it is coming from the God whom he continues to worship and revere—the God who, he now sees clearly, brings tribulations upon both the righteous and the unrighteous. This new knowledge of God is both a revelation and a cause of renewed fear, and Job cries out afresh: "I will speak in the anguish of my spirit, I will complain in the bitterness of my soul."

And complain he does, grumbling aloud that all around him, wicked men are flourishing and rejoicing while he rots in misery. Sadly he recalls his former prosperity, the esteem in which he was held, the pleasure he took in his children and his comfortable life. The contrast between the remembered past and the woe-filled present makes him mourn anew.

Each day, as Job becomes weaker and more gaunt, his friends keep up their long-winded harangues, criticizing him for continuing to maintain that he has lived a good life when obviously he has sinned (if he hadn't sinned, why were all these awful things happening to him?), accusing him of arrogance and pride. Their inability to offer him pity and comfort wounds Job, until he eventually accuses them in turn of being "miserable comforters" and asks them to hold their peace.

At last the day comes when Job sinks so low that he is almost in despair. His body is wasted and wrinkled. He has become a pariah; except for his three friends, whose words lash him, no one will come near him, not even his relatives or his remaining servants. God has taken everything from him, even his hope.

Then another man comes to speak to Job, younger than Eliphaz, Bildad and Zophar, an angry young man named Elihu who, he says, has restrained himself out of respect for the age of the others. He has been bursting to speak, and when he does, his message is more penetrating than any words Job has heard so far.

Why strive against God? Elihu asks Job. God is

not accountable to man; if what he brings about on earth appears to be unjust, it is man's understanding of justice that is flawed, not God's embodiment of it.

Consider for a moment the incomprehensible power and majesty of God, Elihu goes on. This is the God of all creation, of sky and sea, storm and drought, desert and fruitful plain. Surely this great and mighty God knows what he is doing, and Job is wrong in failing to acknowledge the underlying goodness of all that happens, even when it causes suffering.

Elihu tells Job to stop complaining and find the deeper meaning of his bitter experience, the meaning that can come only when he asks God to open his eyes and give him understanding. What he ought to say to God is, "Lord, I have borne your afflictions, I will not offend you any more. Where I fail in understanding, teach me. If I have done wrong, I will not do it again."

Suddenly the scene shifts in the biblical narrative, and the poet has God himself address Job, speaking out of a whirlwind, thundering forth in powerful language that makes Job quake and surrender his querulous protest.

Where were you, Job, when I laid the foundations of the world, God demands, "when the morning stars sang together, and all the sons of God shouted for joy?" Where were you when I made the rain, and divided the waters, measured the depth of the sea and made the heavens? Are you so old that you can remember these things? Or so strong that you can influence them?

Shaken to the core by his encounter with the divine, Job is thoroughly chastened. Up to this time, he says, he has only heard about God, in words; now he sees God with his own eyes, and he is a changed man. "I abhor myself," Job declares, "and repent in dust and ashes."

Now, the poet tells us, "the Lord turned the captivity of Job," and reversed his fortunes. Suddenly his flocks and herds were restored—and so abundantly that he was twice as wealthy as he had been before his losses began. His brothers and sisters gathered around him, and all his acquaintances, and they comforted him and brought him gifts of gold. His health too was restored, so that he lived a very long life, and even had ten more children.

So Job witnessed the power of God three times over: first when he underwent his tribulations, then when he met God and was chastised by him, and finally when he received renewed abundance and wholeness. No doubt the memory of his time of torment, and the grief he felt for the loss of his children, stayed with him for the rest of his life, but both were overshadowed by his awe for the God who had visited him in his affliction and swept it away.

The Mentality of the Afflicted

The vivid and dramatic story of Job, his sharp descent from a plateau of plenty into an abyss of deprivation and pain, then his equally sudden recovery of all that he had lost and more besides, furnishes a model for spiritual autobiography that many people find familiar and compelling. Not everyone has followed the pilgrim way, or sought illumination through an intellectual quest, but nearly every mature adult has known times of loss and hurt, and the anguish that accompanies them.

All too often the losses seem catastrophic, like Job's—that is, they arrive unforeseen, and we are unprepared to contend with the extremes of emotion that they bring in their wake. Sometimes one piece of bad news follows another, and then another, until we begin to wonder if the trend will ever be reversed. Job loss, marital problems, difficulties with children, bankruptcy, bereavement, natural disasters—these and other troubles may descend on us in clusters, leaving us struggling to right the balance of our lives. Illness, physical pain, perhaps a chronic disability may arrive to make our situations even worse.

Out of the depths of our misery, we may, like Job, keep our faith in a higher power that is able to bring healing and relief ("Though he slay me," Job says of God, "yet will I trust him"), or we may groan and complain, as Job did, or we may even ultimately decide that God has abandoned us or that he does not exist.

For a season of loss calls into question our deepest spiritual resources. If we are lucky, the loss is followed by healing and readjustment—and, one hopes, restoration or replacement, in some form, of what has been lost. To have experienced such a cycle of deprivation and recovery can be strengthening, for it gives hope that, when future losses arrive, they too will be followed by gains.

Job suffered in part because he felt hopeless, but we may choose to look on a period of pain and anguish, not as a permanent condition, but as a time of testing. It then becomes one very difficult season in the course of a long life, not a central theme in that life.

Some people, however, adopt the mentality of the afflicted. That is, they form a view of themselves and their lives as in a constant state of adversity. Periods of hardship or loss then are seen as the norm, and times of relief as the exception. Their spiritual stories describe a downward plunge, through a series of ordeals, toward a bottomless pit of failure and despair. They may believe, in their heart of hearts, that they are unworthy of finding their way back to wholeness. Or they may, in their distorted thinking, begin to interpret even positive events in a negative light.

This is the danger of adopting the way of the afflicted as the paradigm of your spiritual autobiography—that instead of finding meaning in your suffering through arriving at a point of repentance and renewal, you become enmired in an overwhelming awareness of victimization from which you cannot escape.

Job's affliction taught him—and us—a valuable spiritual lesson. He learned that he ought never to be complacent when his life was going well, for at any time, without warning, he could lose everything. Yet if he should lose everything, he had to remember that God is always at work, bringing about his incomprehensible will through the terror and complexity of the world, whether his creatures understand his purposes or not.

If, as you ponder the shape of your spiritual autobiography, you feel a kinship with Job, it may be because you have adopted the way of the afflicted as your spiritual world view. You may see hardship on every hand, and you may feel isolated in your suffering. Or you may have had the strengthening experience of passing through a time of sorrow and distress and discovering that your spiritual roots are deep and enduring, and that the power of the spirit within you was available to bring healing and restoration.

EXERCISES:
THE WAY OF THE AFFLICTED
AND YOUR SPIRITUAL STORY

1. Was there a time in your spiritual life when you felt unjustly burdened with suffering? Briefly describe the situation, and your reaction to it.

....

....

....

....

....

....

....

....

....

....

....

....

....

....

....

....

....

2. Have you, in the course of your life, ever felt so overwhelmed by a series of catastrophes that, like Job, you were tempted to despair? What brought back your hope?

....
....
....
....
....
....
....
....
....
....
....
....
....
....
....
....
....
....
....
....

3. Describe if you can the most severe loss you ever experienced (bereavement, loss of friends or of employment, loss of property or possessions, any major loss). What inner resources did you discover at that time? Did your loss turn out to be in any sense a blessing in disguise?

....

....

....

....

....

....

....

....

....

....

....

....

....

....

....

....

....

....

4. Have you ever, like Job, felt isolated and alone, or surrounded by "friends" who offered more criticism or unwanted advice than support? Were you able to find spiritual support at that time?

....

....

....

....

....

....

....

....

....

....

....

....

....

....

....

....

....

....

....

4

THE WAY OF
THE PRODIGAL

$\mathcal{T}$he biblical story of the prodigal son offers yet
another model for writing your spiritual autobiography, one that is both poignant and rich in meaning.

In the fifteenth chapter of the Book of Luke, Jesus
is speaking to a group of worldly men and women,
and tells them this parable. A father had two sons,
very different from each other in their natures. The
firstborn son was dutiful, responsible, and obedient
while the younger son was impulsive and pleasure-
loving, always eager to enjoy himself and notably
lacking in a sense of moderation.

One day the younger son came to his father and
asked that his future inheritance be given to him at
once, as he did not want to wait until it came to him
in the natural course of events. The father agreed,
dividing his possessions and giving the younger son
his share.

Immediately the younger son went away, as far away as he could get, into a "far country," and began spending his inheritance lavishly and recklessly. According to reports that came back to his family, the young man was surrounding himself with low company—prostitutes, inebriates, other spendthrifts like himself and hangers-on who fed at his sumptuous table and drank up his wine.

How long this life of excess continued we aren't told, perhaps months, perhaps years. Long enough, at any rate, to cause an estrangement in the family. The firstborn son was critical of his wayward brother, angry at him for throwing away his portion of their father's money and full of condemnation for his chosen way of life. The younger son, for his part, was well aware that he was breaking every rule by which he had been brought up, and that he was bringing dishonor on himself and his family, especially his father.

Yet he continued to pursue his profligate course, spending more and more, exhausting himself in what the biblical account calls "riotous living," wasting his energies even as he squandered the money in his purse. Finally the day came when his money was gone, and his companions in debauchery, seeing that they could no longer feed at his trough, abandoned him for wealthier patrons.

Now he was alone, and in trouble. For a severe famine spread through the country he was living in, and with his money gone, he was unable to buy what little food there was. So, in desperation, he offered himself as a servant and entered the household of a man of means. He was sent out into his master's fields to feed his pigs.

What a contrast! From being the lord of a lavish establishment, living only for pleasure, surrounded by merrymakers and perpetual feasting and revelry, to wallowing in the mud of a sty, humiliated and hungry, with only the pigs for company. Now the prodigal was suffering, because his master fed him so little that even the husks he threw to the pigs looked appetizing, and he longed to make a meal of them.

Before long the reality of his situation became overwhelmingly clear. He had made a terrible mistake. He had been thoughtless, reckless, foolish. In the words of the biblical account, "he came to himself," and realized what he needed to do to repair his life.

There was no famine in his father's country. If he returned there, he could count on having enough to eat, for he was sure that even his father's lowest servants were fed better than he was. But how could he return, after having thrown away all his father's money? He could not expect to be received as a son, he had forfeited his right to that honorable position. But what if he offered himself as a servant in his father's fields? Surely then he would not be turned away.

Traveling slowly and in great hardship, for the journey was long and he had to rely on charity for his bread, the prodigal son made his way toward home. In his mind he rehearsed the speech he would make to his father when he got there.

"Father," he planned to say, "I have sinned against heaven, and before thee, and am no more worthy to be called thy son. Make me as one of thy hired servants."

At last he came again into his own country, and to the outskirts of his father's lands. As he started along the path leading to his father's courtyard, he must have felt dread, anxiety—and at the same time thankfulness and relief. But he was certainly unprepared for what happened next.

He was still a long way off when he saw a figure running along the path toward him. He watched the man come closer—and realized, to his great surprise, that it was his father. And the expression on his father's face was not one of anger or disapproval, but of great joy and happiness.

His father stretched out his arms, and embraced his prodigal son, kissing him and weeping for joy. And in that moment, before any words were spoken, the prodigal knew that he was forgiven, and the slate was wiped clean, and he was truly home again.

Still, he began to speak the words he had prepared. "Father I have sinned against heaven, and in thy sight, and am no more worthy to be called thy son."

But his father interrupted him, calling to his servants and giving them orders, his voice full of emotion.

"Bring forth the best robe," he instructed them, "and put it on him, and put a ring on his hand, and shoes on his feet." He went on, giving orders about the preparation of a great feast. Fetch the calf we've been fattening up for a special occasion, he said, and slaughter it, and let us eat and celebrate. "For this my son was dead, and is alive again; he was lost, and is found."

The celebrating began almost at once. Musicians were summoned, the calf was killed and dressed and cooked over an open fire. All the household servants busied themselves preparing food and messengers were sent out to invite friends and neighbors to the banquet. Soon the sound of music and dancing could be heard a long way off, even in the fields where the eldest son, who had not been present when the prodigal son returned, was hard at work.

When he heard all the merrymaking the eldest son called to one of the servants and asked what was going on. The servant told him what had happened, how his father was giving a feast to celebrate the safe return of the son he had lost.

Far from being glad that his long-lost brother had

come home, the elder brother was angry and full of resentment. He would not welcome his brother home, in fact he refused to even attend the feast, and stayed out in the field, working as usual.

Eventually his father came out to where he was and talked to him. The eldest son poured out his grievance. I have served you for many years faithfully, he said, and you've never given me a banquet—in fact you've never even given me so much as a goat to kill and eat with my friends. But now that my brother is here, my scandalous, spendthrift brother, who squandered everything you gave him on worthless pleasures, you kill the fattened calf and give a great feast! The implication was clear: the father was being unfair, and the eldest son's years of faithfulness and self-discipline were not being acknowledged.

The father's response was gentle but insistent.

Son, he said, do not begrudge your brother the fattened calf. Everything I have, all my animals, are yours already, and you are always here at my side, sharing my possessions. But our feasting today is appropriate, for something wonderful has happened, and we must celebrate it. Your brother was dead, and now has returned to life; he was lost, and now he is found.

The story ends there, but we may hope that the father invited his eldest son to the banquet, and that in time he learned from his father to forgive, and accept, and embrace the brother who had gone astray but had at last come home.

THE MENTALITY OF THE PRODIGAL

The parable of the prodigal son (or daughter) evokes a strong resonance. Many of us have, like the prodigal, left our roots and gone out into the world, as if to a far country, and, casting off the confining strictures of our upbringing, spent ourselves in pleasure-centered living. Or we have sought, in various ways, to leave our old selves behind—the selves we associate with our family and upbringing—and make or discover new selves in an environment free of constraints or accountability.

We may in time have come to a point, like the prodigal son, where the new life we have built for ourselves begins to seem inadequate, and we feel a need to return to our origins, and to the self we left behind. For the prodigal the spur to his return, the thing that made him come to himself again, was physical hardship, but in many lives it is not any outward event that causes a person to want change but a slow internal process whose beginning may be so subtle that it goes unnoticed.

The pattern for spiritual autobiography offered by the story of the prodigal son is a circle, with one half of the circle representing going outward from the home base and the other half representing the return. In your life you may have "gone full circle" more than once, sometimes returning chastened and humbled, like the prodigal son, sometimes returning enriched by the experience of departing from and returning to the self.

But there is another dimension to this parable of the prodigal son. The story may be read as a departure from the higher spiritual self—the self that seeks to live a balanced, moderate, responsible life of integrity, incorporating body, mind and spirit— and a flight to one's lower nature, to all that is immoderate, heedless, and disjointed. For it was not merely that the prodigal kept unwholesome company, and gave full rein to his sensual appetites; he gave himself up to the forces of entropy—chaos and waste and decay.

If the parable of the prodigal son reminds you of your own spiritual story, it may be that you too have abandoned yourself, at some time in your life, to chaotic, wasteful living that ate away at your strength and threatened to eclipse your spirit. You may have had a battle with addiction or lawbreaking or simply with severe self-indulgence. And you may have found your way out of that destructive way of life and back to home and wholeness.

Or you may, at some point, have known what it is to want to get as far away from home as possible, to leave behind the spiritual self that was molded in your childhood and cast off the constraints of your past. You may have eventually found yourself lost in a spiritual wilderness, and wanted to go home again, to regain some sort of spiritual coherence, either through study or through adopting a formal belief system or beginning a regular spiritual practice.

Or you may have felt alienation from your roots, not through a thirst for independence or a flight into vice but because you were raised in a dysfunctional family. Years later, as a mature adult with an understanding of why your childhood was the way it was, you may want to go home again—not to return to the dysfunction, but to the people you loved and whom you can now forgive.

Another reason this story may appeal to you as a pattern for your spiritual autobiography is that you may have had the wonderful experience of "coming home" to the embrace of divine forgiveness, an experience like no other. The powerful hymn "Amazing Grace" celebrates this remarkable feeling, of being caught up so fully in the force of God's love that all one's wayward past is washed away and the slate is wiped clean. The hymn writer borrowed the words of the parable to make his point. "I once was lost and now am found," he wrote. Like the prodigal, he came home to grace, and was restored to himself.

If you see your spiritual life as a circle describing the loss and recovery of home and self, you may have adopted the mentality of the prodigal son or daughter. If so, you have no doubt learned—or at least been exposed to—valuable lessons about yourself, and no doubt you have grown and matured in consequence. The risk in the prodigal mentality is that you may have a tendency to focus on yourself alone, and to forget the other people in your story. Prodigal people are apt not only to waste their resources, but to waste the people around them, and hence to forfeit their place in the family and in the larger community. (Fortunately, others are often generous and forgiving, and, out of love, will offer a second and a third chance.)

Like the son in the parable, who gave no thought to his father or brother when he set out on his journey to the far country, you may tend to overlook the needs of others in your self-centered wanderings. Because of this, you may miss out on the experience of being needed by those you love, and being able to provide them with what they need most—your time and your attention. The prodigal mentality has difficulty understanding mutuality, altruism, consensus—let alone self-sacrifice.

On the other hand, the prodigal who profoundly comes to him- or herself again and obtains the gift of joyful reincorporation into family and true self has a matchless experience, and finds a joy that only one who was lost can know.

EXERCISES:
The Way of the Prodigal
and Your Spiritual Story

1. Was there a time in your life when you were eager to put as much distance as possible between yourself and your family/spiritual roots in order to carve out a different life for yourself? Write a one-paragraph description of that time.

....

....

....

....

....

....

....

....

....

....

....

....

....

....

....

2. When, if ever, have you been prodigal and wasteful with your time? Your self? Your possessions? Were you left with an empty feeling afterward?

3. Have you ever had the experience of "coming home" to yourself after a long period of absence or alienation? Write a brief description of that time.

....

....

....

....

....

....

....

....

....

....

....

....

....

....

....

....

....

....

....

....

5

WHERE TO START: TAKING INVENTORY

The previous four chapters introduced you to four models for the spiritual autobiography: the meandering journey of Christian the pilgrim, the ascending spiral of Augustine, the sharp drop and recovery of Job, and the circle of outbound and inbound journeying of the prodigal son.

These are only a few of the possible patterns one might adopt, and are meant to serve as a springboard for your own discoveries.

Yet by noticing not only the shape but the characteristics of each of the four models, and the mentality that tends to accompany it, you may have attained some insight into the nature of your own past path.

Before abandoning the models entirely and moving on to construct your own scaffolding for your autobiography, consider using the models in a slightly different way—not as patterns for the entirety of your spiritual life, but as useful ways of viewing certain parts of it. For instance, you may have felt affinities with Job and his tribulations in your twenties, but in your thirties you may have adopted the mentality of the intellectual seeker, and so on.

The important thing is to attempt to get an overview of the general course of your spiritual life, whatever its form or shape, so that you can plot it in a way that is meaningful to you.

Before attempting to do this, you might want to stop for a moment and consider whether yours has been, on the whole, a serene life or a tumultuous one. Has it been a life of calm and orderliness or a life of striving? Your chosen paradigm should reflect these underlying qualities.

WORKSHEET I:
GRAPH OF YOUR SPIRITUAL
LIFE COURSE

Before beginning this worksheet, look back at the first exercise in Chapter 1, where you sketched a rapid overview of your spiritual life as a journey. Now that you have been exposed to several alternate paradigms, and have had some time to think about your life further, draw your life again, in more detail this time, noting important spiritual landmarks or turning points and keeping in mind the dimensions of journeying, intellectual seeking, tribulation, and waywardness. Before you begin, make a conscious choice of a single pattern (meandering line, upward spiral, sharp downward drop and upward ascent, circle, or other pattern you have discovered) and chart the events and seasons of your life along that shape.

Give yourself plenty of time to do this. The more time you spend, the more fruitful and meaningful the process will be.

....

....

....

....

....

THE INVENTORY: YOUR RAW DATA

Now that you have plotted the broad course of your spiritual life, you are ready to begin the process of gathering the material from which to write your life story.

Finding this material can be an absorbing, intriguing process, at times surprising, at times perhaps disturbing, but always instructive. Nearly everyone who investigates his or her past comes up against unexpected discoveries, or makes fresh connections that were never apparent before. Remember, you are not only uncovering new information but putting together what you already know about your past in new ways, so that it takes on a meaningful configuration. You are both researcher and interpreter of your life.

Begin by bringing together as many objective records as you can, baby books, photo albums, school records, important papers, letters, diaries, any written or pictorial evidence that you have saved. You may have a roomful of material or a drawerful, but everything is potentially useful.

Once you have everything together, try to sort it, by year if possible, otherwise by what general season of your past it belongs to.

Using a large notebook, make a memory log, designating one or two pages (or more if necessary) for each year of your life, beginning with the year of your earliest memory. Note down in the log what you can recall about each year. If you find yourself having to leave some years blank or nearly blank, it may help to orient yourself by means of important national or world events: where were you living, what were you doing when Neil Armstrong walked on the moon? when Jimmy Carter was elected? when the Berlin Wall came down?

Enter important family events in your log—births, marriages, divorces, deaths, family reunions, other marking events. If you have pictures of these occasions, look at them closely. Do you look contented? Restless? Relaxed? Stressed? In the center of things or on the margins? These may be clues to your spiritual state of being.

Add to your memory log any major spiritual episodes, brief or prolonged, that you can recall. Include not only such formal occurrences as making a decision to join a religious organization or attending a retreat that influenced you but other important times. For example, you may have recovered from a major illness and during that recovery period you may have begun to reexamine your values and become reacquainted with your spiritual self. Or you may have initiated a career change that had the effect of shifting your priorities noticeably, from an emphasis on high income and high status to an emphasis on service to the community and a greater sense of personal fulfillment.

In making your inventory of spiritual landmarks, be sure to include dark seasons as well as uplifting ones. The bleak years of a failing marriage, times when you knowingly and repeatedly caused pain to others yet felt you could not help yourself, the day you ran away from a religious school at the age of fourteen and swore you would never go near another church for as long as you lived, periods when you wrestled with your conscience or when, to your dismay, you felt that you no longer had a conscience and that you had lost your bearings entirely—these and like experiences belong in your log.

Sometimes the most profound chapters in our spiritual lives happen when we are alone. Those quiet moments when, while taking a walk or watching the moon rise, we receive a private epiphany and a feeling of unearthly joy comes over us, a sense of connectedness to the whole of creation. Times when prayers are answered in such a startlingly direct and immediate way that we are awed and taken aback. Ephemeral feelings that arise when something deep within us is stirred by a memory or a sudden flash of insight. Search your memory for these elusive but meaningful episodes, and add them to your log.

Exercises That Aid in Accessing Your Past

When your memory runs dry, consider trying other ways of tapping into your past:

1. Sit quietly, in a relaxed, comfortable position, and listen to a favorite piece of music. Gently turn your thoughts to an earlier time in your life, and visualize yourself as a child, or as an adolescent, or at any chosen stage of life. Observe the image of yourself that comes into your mind, without judging or criticizing. Note with care how you are dressed, what activities you are engaged in, what your general demeanor is. As you watch your younger self, other images may flow into your mind. Don't force the images, or attempt to direct them. You may be surprised at what emerges. Write any memories or insights into your memory log.

2. Sitting at your word processor or typewriter, or with pen in hand, engage in a written dialogue with your younger self. Ask that self questions. Be patient: in most cases, answers will emerge.

3. Using a technique called "clustering" can trigger buried recollections. Take a large sheet of blank paper and write, in the center, a word that has been impor-

tant in your spiritual past. Words such as "love," "family," "connection," "path," "healing" and "truth" come to mind. Now, as fast as you can, without pausing for conscious thought, write around the initial word as many affiliated words as you can think of, radiating outward. Each word you add can begin a new cluster, until you have built up a wide-ranging, imaginative array of words. In forming that array, you may come across new material for your story.

4. Try autonomic writing. Before beginning this exercise, do your best to put aside any skepticism or fears you may have about this process, trusting that, through the working of the spirit, what comes to you will be in your best interest.

Sit with pen in hand before a blank sheet of paper. Set aside your conscious mind, and allow the pen to move across the paper, perhaps in meaningless lines at first, but eventually forming letters and words. Do not lift the pen off the sheet. As the words begin to come, let them flow freely. Don't censor anything, just become a vessel for the message that is coming through. If you start to write something that disturbs you, you have a choice: you can end the exercise, telling yourself that you will return to it another time, or you can pay close attention to the disturbing material, being as objective about it as you can, realizing that it too is part of your past and that it forms an element in your total story.

FINDING THE TRACKS OF THE SPIRIT

If you have spent the necessary time and brought together as much material as you can from memory, pictures and documents, supplemented by attempts to access buried memories through subliminal means, you will by now have a substantial body of evidence about your past.

But this evidence is not, in itself, a record of the working of the spirit in your life. It is a jumble of facts and intimations, a mosaic of inferences. Your task now is to sift it carefully, looking for the tracks of the spirit.

This is not an easy or obvious task. How do we recognize the workings of the spirit in our lives? Or its absence? Each of us must wrestle with this question on his or her own, but there are certain indications to look for.

One is, simply, the acknowledgment of the spiritual as an important, if not the primary, dimension of our selves. In past centuries this acknowledgment was unquestioned, indeed it was part of the foundation of Western culture. In our own time, at the cusp of the twenty-first century, this is no longer true, although there has been a marked resurgence of interest in and respect for the things of the spirit.

Simple acknowledgment, then, of the existence and significance of the spiritual in our lives is one indicator of an upwelling of the spirit within us.

Awareness of, perhaps a growing preoccupation with, spiritual issues and a distinct focus on them is another. A change in priorities to reflect this awareness is yet another.

As spiritual things move toward the center of our lives, other concerns move toward the periphery. The result may be any or all of the following: the quickening of our spiritual reflexes (being more closely attuned to our deepest purposes in life), spending more time in prayer or meditation, showing greater tolerance, kindness, more humanity toward others, becoming more one-pointed, less fragmented, spending more time pursuing altruistic goals.

It is a paradox that many people find it easier to identify times when the tracks of the spirit were faint or seemingly nonexistent than when they were deep and firm. When the lamp of spirit burns low in our lives, our reflexes become sluggish; we stumble along paths of emptiness, pursuing goals that, though they may be impressive in material terms, ultimately lead to futility. We become disconnected from our higher selves, and yield to self-indulgence and self-importance. We are especially vulnerable to depression, doubt, and fear. We treat others inconsistently, or shabbily.

As you think through the course of your life, watching for signs of spiritual richness and spiritual emptiness, pay attention also to the turning points;

what happened to lift you out of a season of darkness, or to cause you to turn your back on spiritual things?

Keep in mind that the search you have embarked on is endless, and answers are often elusive and slow in coming. Your goal is to become more discerning in observing the working of the spirit in your life. This process of increasing discernment is ongoing, and requires patience and an openness to learning. Meanwhile, carry out the task as best you can, confident that the help you need is always at hand.

EXERCISES:
Questions to Ponder

1. When were you most earnestly seeking spiritual depth, or truth? When were you least concerned with these issues?

....

....

....

....

....

....

....

....

....

....

....

....

....

....

....

....

....

....

2. When were you urgently seeking help from a transcendent source?

....

....

....

....

....

....

....

....

....

....

....

....

....

....

....

....

....

....

....

....

....

3. When were you consciously separating yourself from all things spiritual, angry at God, disillusioned with faith, or cynical about belief? Have you ever thought to yourself that believers in any faith are naive or benighted—that the only reality is the material world?

6

Surveying the Seasons of Your Spiritual Life: I

*N*ow you are ready to embark on writing a preliminary outline of your spiritual autobiography. Unless you have an exceptional facility with words, you will find it easier to break this large task into sections, working on one section at a time. (Of course, this is only one approach to setting down the record of your spiritual life; if you want to pursue another, by all means do so.)

Early Childhood Years

In many ways the richest and most influential time in any person's life is the time most difficult to remember: early childhood, the years from birth to about age seven. The imprint of these early years is indelible; a person's worldview, their understanding and expectations of others and of the divine is shaped by what they learn and observe during these years, and though their opinions may change later, their early grounding will always remain as a strong reinforcement or counterweight to their adult views.

If you are fortunate, your beginning years were spent in a secure and nurturing environment, with steadfast parents who loved you and each other and who taught you as well as showed you that the world is congruent and orderly and that people are basically decent and honorable.

But it may not have been that way. You may have known only minimal security, and little nurture. The household into which you were born may have been full of tensions, with too little love and too much unpredictability and even, at times, injury. Or it may have been loving and secure for part of your early years, and troubled for another part.

These circumstances, whatever they were, formed your spiritual self. Predictably, if you were nurtured and felt safe, you developed a spiritual outlook that assumed a benevolence at work in the universe, and if you felt unsafe, you imagined the universe as a hostile place, full of random harm. Possibly you were taught to pray before you went to sleep each night, a prayer to ward off danger, or you were taught to value the protection of a guardian angel (which implied that there was much that needed to be guarded against). Such early messages form our deepest expectations; their influence is lifelong.

For good or ill, our view of our parents influences our view of God (and the majority of children, whether or not they receive religious training, have a concept of God; it appears to be innate). If you were controlled by a parent's unpredictable, punitive anger, your image of God will probably be, on some level, that of a wrathful deity who cannot be trusted. If you were blessed with at least one patient and affectionate parent your image will be correspondingly benign.

In recent decades fathers have been retreating more and more from their children's lives, either as a result of divorce settlements that place children with their mothers or because women are choosing to bear and raise children on their own, or for other reasons. Perhaps because the divine has (in recent millennia at least) traditionally been imagined as male, the role of the father in spiritual formation is crucial. As you prepare to begin work on your life story, pay particular attention to your father, his personality and treatment of you, and his overall role in your life.

Did you have an actively involved father living with you during your early childhood years? Was he approving? Did he spend a lot of time with you? Was he present in your life yet unavailable, wrapped up in his own concerns or preoccupied with work or outside interests? What messages, tacit or overt, did he convey? How has the presence or absence of your father helped to form your idea of your divine parent?

A child's understanding is primal, but far from simple. Our childhood experience is marked by intense crosscurrents of feeling, strong and enduring impressions, especially in response to losses or family clashes, imaginative flights and fiercely felt loyalties and aversions. These complex feelings and reactions send us reeling, and as young children we lack the ballast and firm anchor of reasoned judgment to guide us through the angry seas of our inner turmoil. In some young lives, early spiritual instruction provides that firm anchor, and a sense of comfort and safety.

Some children, however, raised by parents determined to protect their sons and daughters from the pitfalls of misguided, overzealous religion, with its propensity for mindless credulousness, self-righteous elitism and narrowness of view, are shut out from all training in the things of the spirit, and must founder on their own.

Which were you? What kind of introduction to the spiritual realm did you have—or were you denied any such introduction? Were you raised in a repressively religious environment, intolerant of normal development, where an unhealthy fear of sensuality or free thought on the part of your parents kept you isolated from the world?

Were you confused by the contrast between what you were explicitly told about God and the workings of his love in your family (God is good, you are loved, we all love each other) and the day-to-day reality of conflict and unloving behavior, which led you to envision the divine in an opposite way?

Many children have mystical experiences. Often they do not confide them to an adult, or to each other. If you had such an experience—for example, a dream in which a religious figure or an angel appeared to you, or a strong feeling of a spiritual presence, a sense of detachment or separation from your body, perhaps brought on by physical trauma or emotional or sexual abuse, any unusual event that you can't explain and that would be difficult even to describe, include it in your inventory of early childhood memories.

WORKSHEET II:
OUTLINE/OVERVIEW OF
YOUR EARLY CHILDHOOD

In the space below, summarize your spiritual formation in early childhood, paying particular attention to
significant events and formative influences. (If you
prefer, and you think you are ready, begin your spiritual autobiography in a separate journal, or on your
word processor. If you opt to do this, think in terms of
devoting four or five pages to this portion of your life.)

....

....

....

....

....

....

....

....

....

....

....

....

....

LATER CHILDHOOD

By the age of seven or so, you were beginning to know who you were, discovering your sense of right and wrong, launching yourself on your path of life. You may well have had some formal religious instruction, a grounding in sacred texts, a learning of ritual and memorization of prayers or creeds. You may have been forced to sit, squirming and distracted, through services designed for adults, and some of what was said may have penetrated your inattention.

If you were like most children, you had an interest in the transcendent, which engaged your imagination and your curiosity. Most likely you did not carry this interest as far as Albert Einstein did when he was a child (he made up his own private religion, complete with a divine being, and worshiped this being in ceremonies of his own invention), but you may instinctively have sought to gratify your curiosity outside the realm of formal religious training. Your attempts to do this, and your speculations about spiritual things, together with any significant discussions you may have had on these topics, belong in your outline in Worksheet III.

The realm of the imaginative unseen, the world of fairies and fairy tales, ghosts and spirits, may have haunted your childhood. Fairy tales are based in myth, and myths are often seen as symbols of faith.

In the mythic realm, powers of light and darkness, good and evil, contend for preeminence, with the forces of light invariably triumphant. Heroes and heroines align themselves with powers beyond themselves, and through the aid of these powers, achieve impossible tasks and bring about remarkable rescues.

If you were steeped in these fabulous narratives, they may have influenced your understanding of the things of the spirit and of your place in the cosmos. To the extent that you were frightened by your awareness of an invisible world of vaguely understood, shadowy forms gliding around the periphery of your brightly lit everyday life, you may have envisioned God as the lord of the shadow-world, and yourself as God's hero or heroine, and found comfort in that realization.

Who were your spiritual role models during your childhood? Were you told stories of saints, and did their superhuman feats, their ability to attempt and endure what you couldn't conceive of attempting and enduring, capture your imagination? Or did they strike you as fools or lunatics, so removed from the mainstream of life that they had no relevance for you?

Did you idolize certain adult believers—a kind Sunday School teacher, a compassionate camp counselor, a tough yet gentle football coach—and want to be like them? Or were you more attracted to follow eccentric paths and wayward individuals—rebels, outsiders, skeptics—who seemed exciting and romantic? These affinities offer important clues to the shaping of your spiritual self.

Were your later childhood years smooth and untroubled, or were they disrupted by divorce or separation from loved ones, the death of a parent or a serious illness in the family? Did you have severe conflict with a sibling? Were there intergenerational tensions, or was your family polarized by politics or religion or some other unhealable breach caused by a major dispute?

Did you have to contend with circumstances too deeply traumatizing to talk about? With inward feelings of shame or inadequacy, deep-seated fears of abandonment or a belief that you had been abandoned, a craving for love and acceptance that was never requited (and which, as a child, you may not have even consciously realized), ill-defined yearnings and longings that kept you in a near-constant state of discomfort? Were you systematically bullied or terrorized by other children? Was there sexual abuse in your family, either overt or in the form of a damaging emotional undercurrent?

If any of these things assailed you, you may have taken psychological refuge in believing that you had a spiritual ally—that, in the language of the Bible, "if God be for us, who then can stand against us?" God became, for you, your partner in the sky, and you may have formed a profound bond with this saving deity who protected you in a time of great stress.

Unless you were kept entirely insulated from the world, you began, in your later childhood years, to glimpse (or possibly even be immersed in) the larger, more raw adult reality, with its violence and seaminess. You encountered uncontrolled passions, sordidness, deceit and betrayal, debauchery and waste. You felt within yourself, not only the tug of immorality, but the lure of pleasure, and the everpresent enticement of temptation. These episodes belong in your spiritual story.

Some children lead rich and secret inner lives, involving a startling array of thoughts and behaviors that depart radically from the sanitized, conventional view of childhood many adults cling to. Children can be self-sacrificing, noble, great-hearted beyond their years, but they can also be brutal, vengeful, even vicious; their fierce loyalties can lead them into criminality. If they are spiritually precocious, they may go to extremes in attempting to mortify their flesh or make themselves worthy through deprivations.

Whatever the shape of your childhood, write an outline or overview of it in Worksheet III.

WORKSHEET III:
OUTLINE/OVERVIEW OF
YOUR LATER CHILDHOOD

With your focus on ages seven to twelve, summarize your spiritual autobiography, keeping in mind the overall pattern you believe best suits your experience. As a child, were you a little pilgrim, a little seeker, a little victim of affliction, a little prodigal son or daughter? What events or influences were formative? Looking back over your later childhood, where can you observe the tracks of the spirit?

....

....

....

....

....

....

....

....

....

....

....

....

....

ADOLESCENCE

It is customary in autobiographical writing to dwell longer on childhood and adolescence than on later seasons of life, and for a good reason: these early years are exceptionally rich in emotional experience, and offer a ripe field for spiritual growth, regression or turmoil.

Adolescence has been aptly called a molting season; the old pelt of childhood is cast off, leaving a raw new self underneath—a self still juvenile, but with abundant signs that a new coat is about to emerge. One of the marks of the new self is spiritual searching. In the years from thirteen to nineteen or so our psychological world expands, we embrace deeper and more complex ways of being human, including exploring (or consciously rejecting) our spirituality.

It is not uncommon for a twelve- or thirteen-year-old to stop attending whatever religious institution he or she has been part of, after weighing its teachings and finding them wanting. Alternative allegiances beckon. Adolescents are especially prone to conversion experiences, and may be converted out of formal religion into a veneration for a sports hero (or the sport itself), or for a political ideology, or for an atheistic system of thought. Any coherent lens through which the world may be viewed offers a challenge to traditional spirituality.

If, as adolescents, our awareness of the world expands, so do our hearts. Hormones race, and desire, with its promise of blissful union, and its danger of heartbreak, crashes over us with the fury of a tidal wave. For a time, this overwhelming awareness of human love may threaten to eclipse whatever we may know of divine love, or the two may become hopelessly and confusingly intermingled. That "oceanic feeling" of being in love, the sense of merging with a vast and all-embracing immensity, has a spiritual dimension; through it we may glimpse a larger and more enduring union with the divine.

Our minds too expand in the teen years. Learning takes place on a larger scale, we take on scope as well as skills. For some, the romance of ideas can be almost as powerful as a romance of the heart, and can open a pathway to a future vocation.

In the later teen years, our horizons widen, faraway places seem irresistibly inviting. The prospect of adventure, the excitement of leaving home and striking out on one's own glimmer with promise.

Yet the more expansive our lives become, the more challenge we take on—and with challenge, risk. If the principal task of adolescence is to discover one's own identity, that cluster of defining characteristics that make one different from the millions of other young people who are also racing toward the threshold of adulthood, then the abundance of new knowledge accumulated during the adolescent years can actually be as unsettling as it is enriching.

Learning about cultures and belief systems that differ widely from our own calls into question comfortable certainties. Becoming able to see one's own spiritual tradition, not as eternal and universal, but as a human creation, timebound and limited to a certain geographical area, shakes one's assumptions and may bring with it a sense of personal confusion. For college students, the razor of intellectual analysis may slash away at our deepest beliefs, making them seem simplistic and lacking in subtlety, without offering any thoughtful or nurturing alternatives.

It is no wonder, given the emotional, sexual and intellectual maelstrom in which we spend our teen years, and the strain on family relations that our transformation brings about, that we are at times overwhelmed and seek escape—into music, into sensuality, into drugs. Some seek the ultimate escape, into oblivion.

What was your experience during adolescence? How did you face and ultimately pass its strenuous tests? How did your spiritual self fare? Use Worksheet IV to outline your life from age thirteen to about age nineteen.

WORKSHEET IV:
OUTLINE/OVERVIEW OF
YOUR ADOLESCENCE

Write an outline or overview of your spiritual autobiography from age thirteen to age nineteen. How did your attitudes toward the things of the spirit change during this time? What new doors were opened for you, and under what circumstances? Were you able to embrace your changing self eagerly, or was the transition painful and difficult?

....

....

....

....

....

....

....

....

....

....

....

....

....

....

7

SURVEYING THE
SEASONS OF YOUR
SPIRITUAL LIFE: II

EARLY ADULTHOOD

*F*ull of vigor and confidence, we plunge into the swift currents of adulthood in our twenties, unhampered by experience, undaunted by the challenges we face. At no other time do we feel so independent, so capable of solving on our own whatever problems may arise. For many people in this season of life, the things of the spirit begin to seem remote, unnecessary, inappropriate to the earthly tasks at hand.

Finding work, moving ahead in a career, toiling through graduate school, running a business, settling down, starting a family, becoming part of the community mainstream—or creating an alternative to it—these endeavors take all the energy we have, and leave little time for contemplation or cultivation of the spiritual life. Besides, it feels as though we, not some remote divine force, make the world run; it is our effort, our vision of the future, our sheer drive and will that power our lives. The more aggressively we throw ourselves into day-to-day activity, the more we are inclined to put the things of the spirit up on a shelf—not quite out of sight, but out of the way, so that we leave ourselves a clear field of action.

Alternatively, we may enter the adult arena having cast off, or gradually turned away from, any allegiance to the realm of the spirit, deciding once and for all that the domain of faith belongs to childhood and is not appropriate for a sophisticated adult. Or we may continue to acknowledge that life has a spiritual dimension, while resolutely turning our backs on all institutional embodiments of it.

After all, it is perhaps the cardinal discovery of adulthood that the world is not run along spiritual lines; in small and large ways, all too many of the people we rub up against bend the rules and dishonor their agreements and exploit and take advantage of one another daily if not hourly. The taint of corruption is never far to seek, and we are urged, if not to lie outright, then to misrepresent, distort and veil the truth, and to hide our true selves as well in order to get ahead, or get along, or, in some instances, get even.

If you were lucky, you never had to face the pressure to compromise your spiritual values. But perhaps you had other pressures—to drink to excess, or take drugs, or to go into debt to support a style of living you couldn't afford. Family tensions or crises may have eaten into your sense of well-being, along with the stress of competing at work or coping with an unhappy marriage or with an uneasily evolving sense of self.

As you left your twenties behind and entered your thirties, you may have begun a new "molting" process like the one you underwent in adolescence, and the resulting change in you may have led to inner strains or to marital or family conflict.

Among the most significant changes that can happen in early adulthood comes about when we begin to ponder the issue of what, if any, spiritual formation we want to give our children. After all, it is one thing to make a decision, as an adult, to put spirituality into the background of our lives, but it is quite another to make that decision on behalf of our children. Children ask questions about ultimate things: God, death, birth, right and wrong. Should they be given the answers religious institutions offer, along with some grounding in sacred texts and ritual? Should they be taught to worship?

In the course of coming to grips with this question, we encounter our own spiritual certainties, or our lack thereof, and this provides an opportunity for a fresh consideration of the role of the spiritual in our lives.

Meanwhile, other circumstances may prompt such a consideration. As the years pass, the futures we endeavor to build with such eager self-confidence may go awry, or turn out to take bafflingly different shapes from those we had hoped for. Life may well present us with the unexpected shocks and jolts of financial difficulty, illness in the family, unanticipated emotional hurdles. Or we may have the disillusioning experience of fulfilling our dreams—only to discover that the price was too high, or the inner rewards too scanty. Such disruptions and surprises are reminders that, however carefully we plan and however energetically we labor, our lives hurtle along paths that are outside our control.

As you look over your early adulthood, what spiritual continuities and disruptions can you perceive? What patterns emerge? Keep these in mind as you make out Worksheet V.

Worksheet V:
Outline/Overview of Your Early Adulthood

Write a summary of your spiritual life in your twenties and early thirties, keeping in mind both the broad pattern you detect and important events or landmarks. (If you prefer, proceed to the writing of your spiritual autobiography in a separate notebook.)

....

....

....

....

....

....

....

....

....

....

....

....

....

....

....

....

MIDLIFE

"In the midpoint of this our life, I lost my way in a dark wood. . . ." So begins a famous account of a spiritual journey, Dante's *Divine Comedy*. The mid-thirties, roughly the midpoint of life, are often a stormy season. Many of us, like Dante, lose our way and enter a private purgatory of uncertainty. Passing from the last years of our extended youth into the unknown territory of midlife, with the weighty term of middle age clearly in view, we pause to get our bearings—and have trouble locating them.

Just at this time, the demands of work are likely to be escalating, and we must confront the uncomfortable issue of precisely how far we have come along the road to success—however we define success. For many people, reminded of the limitations of their achievements, and humbled (or frustrated) by the prospects before them, soul searching sets in, particularly if thorny family issues have arisen to complicate the present and make us worry for the future.

For the mid-thirties are also a time when family demands escalate. For some, unexpected issues arise: a beloved child rebels, or begins to develop into a person we continue to love but do not like; a marriage enters a barren and cheerless season; divorce arrives, and in its aftermath come the burdens of single parenthood or the stark new terrain of singlehood, and with it, the apprehensive feeling of having to start over.

In meeting these challenges we may grow spiritually, or we may stagnate, lose heart, and regress. Even if things are going smoothly, a certain heaviness may set in in midlife, a feeling of being enmired in the everydayness of things.

In the decade of the forties, if we are lucky, fresh shoots may spring forth from the mature tree. Having passed through the crisis period of the mid- to late thirties, and perhaps feeling a sense of satisfaction at having weathered that test of mettle, our lives may take on a new energy. If we are aware of having called on our spiritual resources during the difficult times, there may arrive a gratifying sense of having won out, a new assurance that whatever life hands us, we have on call the strength to endure and the tenacity to overcome.

Midlife may bring particular satisfactions—financial security, a stable and lasting marriage (or a second or third marriage that finally feels right), the reaching of career milestones or the arrival of pleasurable new opportunities in work, the rewards of recognition and widening personal influence. If we are flourishing in both our personal and professional lives, we may feel justly pleased that we have lived long enough, and done well enough, to have made a small contribution to the betterment of the world.

If you have reached or passed midlife, what do

you look back on as you search for the signs of the spirit? Did you come through a dark passage and out into the sunlight again? Or are you currently facing uncertainties and anxieties? Have you known the deep satisfaction of hearing a child thank you for the good parent you've been, and of watching that child take his or her place in the world with grace and competence?

When you think back over this season of your life, have there been times when you came to a crossroads and had to make a moral choice? Are you proud of the choice you made? Can you perceive the working of the spirit at that choice point? Are you aware of times when you seemed to gather strength, and other times when you felt enfeebled?

Gradual enfeeblement is, like it or not, a theme of midlife. Youthful strength wanes, youthful beauty passes, emotional resilience too may wither, to be replaced by a less tolerant, more curmudgeonly self we hardly recognize. The slow sapping of our powers and our most desirable outward attributes is yet another test of fortitude, as are the onslaughts of ill health that often give us pause in midlife.

For women, the onset of menopause, with its distressing and exhausting physical assaults and its equally unnerving hormonal fluctuations, can be a shock; a new and less attractive face greets us in the mirror, and we feel an unfamiliar surge of aggressive energy, while lamenting added girth and lowered stamina. To fully accept this alteration in our sense of self requires a significant adjustment.

Sometime in midlife, most of us become orphans. The death of our parents is not only a major loss in itself, it signals a generational shift that makes us the new matriarchs and patriarchs of the clan. And although in a youth-oriented culture such as that of America, seniority carries primarily symbolic weight, still, in terms of how we feel inside, the alteration is a major one.

It has been said that when one's parents die, there is no longer any line of defense between oneself and death. Mortality looms, immense and overawing and inescapable. Now spiritual issues take on fresh significance, the search for meaning in life is quickened and along with it the search for a new identity, one that, perhaps for the first time, acknowledges the dimension of the spirit.

It is no wonder that in midlife, many people begin a spiritual search for the first time, or return to their spiritual roots. Those who have been faithful to a lifelong form of worship or practice may experience a deepening of that commitment, or a breakthrough to a new level of empowerment or a renewed sense of the value of the spiritual connection.

Conversion experiences are not uncommon. The increasing urgency of midlife issues may set in motion a fresh assessment of what matters and what doesn't, what we now need that we didn't when we were younger. With maturity we gain the independence to investigate belief even if those we associate with have no interest in the things of the spirit or even feel contemptuous of others who do.

For some people, however, midlife is the season in which spiritual things are laid aside—seemingly for good. Convinced by their life experience that there is nothing beyond the material world, they gather their forces for the last stage in life's journey, a stage they intend to traverse alone.

WORKSHEET VI:
OUTLINE/OVERVIEW OF MIDLIFE

Summarize your spiritual life from about age thirty-five to sixty, paying particular attention to the satisfactions and challenges these years have brought, or may be bringing you currently. Did you ever lose your way? Have you grown spiritually? Have you experienced in any sense a return to your spiritual roots?

....

....

....

....

....

....

....

....

....

....

....

....

....

....

....

....

LATE MATURITY AND ELDER YEARS

In some cultures it is customary for people reaching the end of midlife to leave most of their material comforts behind and seek out a more austere and meditative environment—to withdraw in order to deliberately cultivate their spiritual selves and devote the rest of their lives to contemplation and quietness.

Our culture does not prepare us for that experience, yet many of us, too, as we reach late middle age, feel an obscure yearning for quiet and simplicity—the tug of the spirit—and wonder how best to answer that call.

And at the same time we feel another impulse, one that on the surface seems contrary to the pull toward asceticism and withdrawal from the mainstream of everyday life. It is the call to give back, pass on, hand down what we have learned—to have closer contact with young people and share with them our store of experience.

How we value that experience depends partly on whether we view our lives as well or ill spent—a judgment calling for spiritual discernment. If you are sixty or older, do you look back over the course of your life with an overall sense of satisfaction and accomplishment, or do you feel a sense of incompleteness or waste? Do you feel like the prodigal son or daughter who has squandered his or her inheritance? Can you imagine a divine voice saying "This is my beloved child, in whom I am well pleased?"

The years from sixty on can be a time of abundant spiritual harvest, a season of ingathering when our storehouses are full—or a season of spiritual famine. It is in either event a time of reckoning, the ultimate opportunity for taking the measure of our lives.

For this reason, as you survey your years past sixty, you have an extraordinary responsibility—and an extraordinary opportunity. You are in a unique position to draw together, in your memory and imagination, all the various strands of your life and observe the pattern they make. No one else can do this, for you alone know your inward and outward history.

Although we are fortunate to live in an era of increased longevity, when living to be a hundred years old or older is no longer rare, mortality inevitably overshadows all that we do and think in this last season of life. We must come to terms with the ultimate loss—the loss of our own continuity, our own consciousness. However we may seek to avert our awareness from it, we know that we must die—perhaps soon, perhaps not for many years.

It is only within the last century that death has become something shameful, to be hidden away, sanitized as much as possible, and above all not to be mentioned. If spoken of at all, it must be veiled in euphemisms. We have lost a sense of the starkness of death, its utter finality. But to the extent that we have lost this harsh truth, we have also lost something important—the understanding of death as a rounding out of life, a natural final chapter in our story. How we approach and experience that final chapter, how we come to terms with our mortality, gives important clues to the spiritual meaning of our lives.

Just as a full realization of the magnitude of death gives a keener sense of value and clarity to life, and allows us to appreciate how precious our term of days on earth is, so an acceptance of the inevitability of dying offers us a chance to do important spiritual work in our last years or decades. Knowing with greater urgency that our time is finite, we can make a more conscious effort to devote a significant part of what time remains to pursuits that are worthwhile, rather than to a shallow pursuit of pleasure, or a private nursing of grievances, or some other self-centered activity.

How do you look on your own mortality? Do you have difficulty admitting it? If you are able to do so, do you envision your death as the end of your pilgrimage? As the ultimate stage in your progress toward spiritual discernment? As an affliction, or, depending on your concept of an afterlife, as a gateway to an ancitipated reward? Or as the great and final homecoming?

To be sure, the approach of mortality brings with

it, not only a shift of viewpoint, but for many people, major challenges: pain and chronic illness, financial concerns (it is still true that the majority of American women die alone, in poverty), loneliness, the decline of a spouse, the death-in-life of Alzheimer's, multiple bereavements. If you live into your eighties or nineties, chances are that you will face the loss of many of your peers, possibly even the loss of one or more of your own children.

It is a cruel paradox of aging that, as we lose strength, the emotional and physical demands on us seem to become heavier instead of lighter. Now, if ever, our spiritual selves are tested as well. Whatever strength of spirit we have garnered over the years rises to meet the challenges—or we sink under their combined weight. The spirit may be willing, but the flesh may be too weak to respond.

For some who have never, throughout their lives, sought to explore their spiritual selves, the years after age sixty may be a time of discovery and empowerment. However they are brought to the point of acknowledging the spiritual dimension of their lives, once that acknowledgment is made, new wellsprings of endurance, fortitude and tenacity become available.

Among the most important tasks of the last season of life is that of reconciliation and forgiveness. Wherever possible, even if only in our own minds, we need to heal rifts, bind up old wounds and make amends. This is part of the wholesome rounding out of our lives, and it is, essentially, a spiritual task. A focus on making whole what was broken may help to keep at bay the tendency to become curmudgeonly as we age, and will certainly bring a greater sense of peace and acceptance for the future.

It is to be hoped that the effort of writing your spiritual autobiography can become an act of reconciliation with your own past, and of self-forgiveness, as well as an opportunity for insight.

WORKSHEET VII:
OUTLINE/OVERVIEW OF LATE
MATURITY AND ELDER YEARS

Write a summary of your years after sixty. Are you aware of the amplitude of your spiritual harvest? How would you assess it? How has the awareness of your own mortality affected the way you have spent your later years? Are you better able now than in the past to draw together the threads of your life and see it as a coherent whole? Are you able to look back at your life with an attitude of acceptance, or are you still at odds with your past? If you were to write your spiritual epitaph, how would it read?

....

....

....

....

....

....

....

....

....

....

....

8

GLIMPSES OF
THE INFINITE

 $\mathcal{T}$ he spirit manifests itself in our lives in a multitude of ways, some highly unexpected, some unfathomable. Some lives contain events and ordeals so far outside what we think of as the norm of human experience that they offer unique glimpses of the everpresent mystery of the divine.

Atypical, larger-than-life episodes, truly harrowing personal challenges, encounters with the force of the spirit so momentous—and sometimes so indescribable—that they seem to lie in another realm entirely than that of day-to-day routine: these too belong in a spiritual autobiography, along with the more conventional matter of our lives, for to leave them out or fail to take a full account of them obscures the truth of our experience and diminishes its breadth and range.

Quite often people who live through extraordinary

times or go through remarkable episodes are reluc-
tant to speak about them, for a variety of reasons.
They may mistrust their own perceptions, or they
may fear for their sanity or fear the mistrust of others or their condemnation or ridicule. They may feel
survivor's guilt, or shame, or simply discomfort. Or
they may be confused and uncertain about how to
treat such uncommon experiences within the larger
framework of their lives.

However private, however hard to grasp, still less
write about, these singular, often unwieldy episodes
have their place in your spiritual history—especially
if, through them, you have been granted a glimpse
of the infinite.

MYSTICAL ENCOUNTERS

Into some lives there come moments so full of awe
and glory that they seem to stand outside time.
Those who experience them are never the same
afterward; it is as if their lives are shattered, and
must be reassembled around the fact of those aston-
ishing moments.

Many people experience photisms, light-visions, in
which they feel themselves to be full of light, or
made of light, their bodies seeming to dissolve into
an incorporeal light-essence. Or they perceive the
room they are in to be flooded with a blinding white

light, which seems to them to be a visitation from a divine source.

Those who undergo such phenomena say that they are all but indescribable—that words cannot begin to capture their essence. They speak of a "brilliant darkness," a "tremor of bliss," a flash or hint of something hidden, yet visible. Often accompanying the photism is a feeling that some knowledge has been imparted, or insight gained. Photisms are brief; they may recur, but each instance is short-lived. And they are entirely outside the control of the observer—no act of will can make them occur.

People who experience photisms may conclude that they have had a brush with the holy—with that compelling, shiver-inducing presence that lies outside all explanation or definition. This presence may be sensed in various ways—sometimes by a perception of light, sometimes by a sense that a strong wave of energy is passing through the body, jolting it awake. The feeling of being in the near presence of a powerful spiritual force appears to be a surprisingly common, though infrequently discussed, occurrence.

Visionary experiences are also surprisingly common. Whether the vision occurs in a dream, or in a dreamlike waking state, the person sees an image of a religious figure, and the sight transforms their lives.

There is a long tradition in Western spirituality of

direct apperceptions of God, whether through sight or hearing or in some other, ineffable way. The German mystic Meister Eckhart wrote of entering "the abyss without mode and without form of the silent and waste divinity"—a sufficiently opaque phrase which reminds us how such encounters do not lend themselves to articulate expression. Yet one does not have to be an exalted spiritual personage, or a hermit withdrawn from the world and committed to living in search of the beatific vision, to encounter the divine.

To be sure, genuine mystical experiences are not to be confused with hallucinations, or drug-induced trances, or flights of the imagination brought on by wishful thinking or dabblings in the occult. Some people who see visions or hear voices are mentally ill, and need to seek treatment. But because we associate these phenomena with a loss of sanity, that should not make us unreceptive to those visitations that instinct tells us are holy.

If you have had encounters such as those described above, your spiritual autobiography is the ideal place to record and explore them. Try, if you can, to integrate these experiences with the rest of your spiritual life; if not, simply describe them as best you can, including all your sense impressions and any feelings that arise. If you are uncomfortable attempting to interpret these episodes, then don't attempt to—but by the same token, resist the temptation to rationalize or underemphasize what you have been witness to. All of your experience is valid, from the standpoint of your own perceptions.

It may be helpful, when pondering extraordinary spiritual events, to imagine that there is, in the most profound recesses of your spirit, a threshold between the finite and the infinite; possibly you have had the good fortune to cross that threshold, if only for a moment. It may also be helpful to read the works of the great mystics, to place your experience within a broader context and make it seem less baffling and more consistent with one current in the mainstream of spiritual history.

Survivors' Tales

As you review the course of your life, you may look back on one episode that, in its magnitude and significance, overshadows all others. Perhaps you had a brush with death, either in a near-fatal accident or in the course of a grave illness. Perhaps you found yourself in extreme circumstances—trapped in a collapsed building, or adrift without a working radio on a disabled boat in the middle of the Pacific, or lost in the wilderness without a map. Perhaps you were a prisoner of war, or a kidnap victim, or under attack.

What all these ordeals have in common is that

they provide us with an opportunity to confront what is deepest and strongest within us, to discover what we are truly made of. And what we discover is that, at our core, we are more than flesh and blood: we are spirit.

Among the most powerful of modern survivors' tales are those that come out of World War II. Concentration camp inmates who were starved, beaten, worked nearly to death, their humanity assaulted in every conceivable way, lived to write of their all but unimaginable ordeals. Their accounts bear witness to the enduring resilience made possible by the up-welling of the spirit.

If you have lived through a severe trial or test (or are currently undergoing one), or have endured cataclysmic events, you may have remained silent about your experience, either because it was (or is) too painful, too searing, or because you have chosen to wall off that part of your life in self-protection. Having walked into the fiery furnace and come out unscathed, you have an urge to put that part of your life behind you permanently, and never to look back.

Yet to disconnect from your cruelest tribulations is to lose the benefit of contacting the strongest, most unquenchable part of yourself. Rather than forfeit this vital connection, make an effort to record your experience in your spiritual story, in as much detail as you can. It may well be that the act of disclosing on paper what you have until now held only in memory will bring you relief and healing. Chances are that, as you write them down, your memories will order themselves more coherently, increasing your understanding of your ordeal and giving you a greater sense of completion and clarity about it.

As you consider how to integrate your most significant episode into your spiritual autobiography, consider the advantages it has brought you. It has taught you a sense of proportion; having undergone such a critical time of testing, you will keep the everyday difficulties and annoyances of life in proper perspective. And it has taught you to trust in the working of the spirit within you to buoy you up in any future catastrophe.

To be sure, many people who survive traumatic circumstances, especially those in which others lost their lives, feel guilty. Survival becomes almost as much of a burden as it is a blessing, because it seems to carry such a heavy responsibility with it. The challenge of this responsibility, and how you bear up under it, are an important part of your spiritual story.

PERSONAL TRAUMAS

We live in a time when even the ugliest human situations—incest, infanticide, murder of parents by children, children murdering other children—are laid bare and made the subject of public discussion. Incidents and circumstances once hidden behind a veil of decency or gentility are now thrown into stark relief.

Yet understandably, family members affected by such tragedies are reticent to talk about them. If you find yourself among the very large number of people whose lives hold such personal traumas, you may be pondering whether—or how—to include them in your spiritual autobiography.

If you are a victim of a traumatic experience, or repeated traumatic experiences, your ordeal may have made you question whatever spiritual beliefs you hold. Or you may feel that you were able to endure your experience only because of your beliefs. If you were not a victim, merely a witness to ongoing tragic events in your family, you may be wrestling with other issues: your desire for revenge, or to see justice done or make restitution, your hope (which may seem futile) for an end to the traumatic circumstances and for forgiveness and ultimate reconciliation.

Such deepgoing and complex episodes, which may well lead to hundreds of hours of thought, prayer, and perhaps therapy—not to mention court appearances and legal conferences—cannot easily be encompassed in a few brief pages; realizing this, you may be tempted to omit them from your spiritual story, possibly imagining that you might either treat them in a separate narrative or leave them unrecorded.

It is precisely because of the far-reaching nature of such traumatic events that you need to write about them, carefully and accurately, making certain that no one else could be harmed by your private revelations. Confide to paper your grief, your fury, your sense of outrage, your frustration, as well as your hope and faith in a positive outcome—whatever you may feel.

If the intensity of your emotions makes it hard for you to express them, or to write about the events that led to them, in a straightforward way, then approach them obliquely. Try describing what happened, and how you felt about it, in a letter to a dear friend. Try writing poetry—not the kind that rhymes, but the kind that distills a mood or an attitude through images and terse phrases. Try writing prayers, or, if the prayers won't come, write curses—whatever unblocks you and allows the story to gush forth.

There may be, in your past, matters between you and your conscience—secret things known to no one but yourself with which you need to come to terms. Perhaps you injured someone, or acted cruelly, or thoughtlessly. You may have committed a crime, or a series of crimes, for which you were never punished. You may have done something that, while not illegal, was morally wrong or resulted in harm. Your spiritual autobiography is a place to admit these things and attempt to put them into the longer perspective of your lifelong relationship with your spiritual self.

You may be among those who, as they read these words, are facing the anguish of a diagnosis of terminal illness. You may or may not be in pain, but you know that the time allotted to you is short and that you may have to endure severe pain as it ebbs.

For you, the task of writing your spiritual life story has particular meaning. Whatever emotional havoc your diagnosis has caused you, it has no doubt sharpened your focus and made the remaining time very precious. In your desire to make the most of that time, you are thinking about summing up your past, and giving it shape and coherence. In its spiritual dimension you find the meaning you seek—and with it, a means of making anguish and suffering comprehensible, and hence easier to bear.

However harrowing your personal trauma may be, it is well to remember that sometimes it takes a catastrophe to bring us face-to-face with our deepest selves—and through them, with the divine that is within us.

WORKSHEET VIII:
EXTRAORDINARY SPIRITUAL
EXPERIENCES

Have you ever had a light-vision or some other astounding experience that left you with the feeling that you were standing in the presence of the holy? Have you ever had a vision of a religious figure? Relate your encounter briefly.

....

....

....

....

....

....

....

....

....

....

....

....

....

....

....

Have you undergone a catastrophic trial or test of endurance? Did this experience deepen your awareness of your spiritual self? Has your survival been burdensome in any way?

Are you carrying secrets concerning family relation-
ships, or are there things on your conscience, which
you would benefit by disclosing? If you are not ready
to write a full narrative of these episodes, name them
here, as briefly as you like. If you could be certain
that no one would ever read what you write, what
would you say about these matters?

9

YOUR SPIRITUAL AUTOBIOGRAPHY: THE ART OF THE POSSIBLE

𝒩ow that you have spent some time thinking about the overall shape of your spiritual story, gathering the material from which it will be written, and systematically looking back over your past in an effort to harvest memories, you are ready to begin writing—if you have not done so already.

You are to be congratulated, at the outset, for undertaking this work. Most people live unexamined lives; you have decided to examine yours, and to record your findings. As you do so, you will uncover surprising rewards.

FORM AND STYLE

When you begin your storytelling, don't be overly concerned with how "finished" or accomplished your narrative is. If you are sincere, if you write from the heart and are true to your memories and feelings about them, chances are you will produce a compelling and readable testimony to your past.

If you think of what you are writing as a work in progress, like your life itself, it will remove some of the pressure of perfectionism.

To be sure, if you can't spell and have only a vague sense of grammar, your writing will be much harder to read, and you will be handicapped in giving full range to your inner voice, because the ability to write complex sentences and to express nuances of meaning through a large vocabulary contribute a great deal to self-expression. The desire to write your spiritual autobiography may be your opportunity to broaden your literary education and acquire new skills.

It may bring you inspiration to read good models of spiritual autobiography—consult your library and bookstore for suggestions—and don't let them intimidate you!

Keep in mind that only you can tell your own story, and only you know how to tell it. You are the ultimate authority, and the ultimate literary guide, to your own past.

If you find that it helps you, try making an outline before you begin. Keeping in mind the overall design of your spiritual life, as you envision it, list the large themes you want to emphasize, and the topics that shed light on each theme. You may want to change your outline as you go along, or ignore it entirely when inspiration strikes.

If you find yourself writing much more about some parts of your spiritual life than others, see if you can discover the reason for this. The tendency itself may be meaningful. Remember, most autobiographers devote at least as much space to their childhood and adolescence as they do to their adult life. So if you find yourself lingering over your early years, you are in good company.

THE WRITING PROCESS

Find a quiet place to work, well lit and with plenty of room to spread out computer, notepad and pens, notes and books. If you are able to set aside long stretches of uninterrupted time in which to compose your spiritual autobiography, you are very fortunate, and your work will benefit; otherwise, make the best of what time your life allows you.

Let others know that you are engaged in a serious task and that you need privacy and peace in which to accomplish it. This means freedom from interruptions, even though for many of us, life seems to be made up of interruptions, and we accomplish whatever we accomplish in the intervals between them.

Because writing engages not only the mind but the body, you may find it useful to warm up to your writing task by exercising. A long walk or jog, a swim or bicycle ride are good ways to wake up your thinking and get you started with zest. To help you detach from the stresses and preoccupations that distract your focus, try relaxation exercises or meditation before you sit down to work.

Honor your own method of working, whatever that may be. If you work best in the morning, set aside time to be at your desk then; if peaceful afternoons are more productive for you, shift other obligations to the morning hours so that your afternoons are free. Some people write best late at night or very early in the morning. Experiment and see which are your best writing hours.

A lot of clichés circulate about writing and writers, most of which, you will find with experience, belong in the realm of myth: that the best writers are always neurotic or addiction prone, that writing is agony, that "all writing is rewriting," and that the elusive perfect sentence requires dozens of drafts. In actuality, many fine writers are well-adjusted, normal people living normal lives. Writing, like most tasks, is sometimes demanding, sometimes uncomplicated, sometimes effortless. While some writers do multiple drafts, many others take care (though not excessive care) with one definitive draft, and never rewrite anything.

There is a mystery to the writing process, and it has affinities with the greater mystery of the working of the spirit in our lives. No one knows where inspiration comes from, or when it is likely to arrive. You may receive your best insights about your spiritual life, not while sitting at your desk, but between pitches on the softball field, or while driving to the mall or standing in line at the supermarket. An especially revealing, well-turned paragraph may come to you, fully formed in your mind, in an idle moment as you sit quietly paying bills or resting or reading. The creative process cannot be understood or tamed; without warning, at any time, lights go on in your mind, bells ring, unexpected epiphanies arrive.

Having said this, it is well to keep in mind that writing can be frustrating (if you have an unproductive day, don't fret, but forgive yourself and let it go; tomorrow will probably be better), boring (if what you are writing causes your mind to wander and makes you yawn, that is a sure sign your narrative is dragging; abandon it and return to the last interesting part), painful (you may be forced to admit things about yourself that wound your pride and chasten your ego), even dangerous (you may unleash long-denied passions).

Don't be surprised if, when you come to the end

of your spiritual autobiography, it tells a different story than the one you thought it would tell. As one exceptionally gifted autobiographer, Bertrand Russell, remarked about his labors, "the things one says are all unsuccessful attempts to say something else."

BLOCKS TO WRITING

What if, in the course of your writing, discouraging thoughts arise to dissuade you? You may imagine that your life is not eventful or valuable enough to write about, or that your skills are not adequate to the task, or you may worry that somehow your manuscript will fall into unsympathetic hands.

Once such worries come to the surface, they tend to multiply, until they paralyze you. But they can be counteracted. Tell yourself that the purpose of writing your spiritual autobiography is not to be able to boast about how significant your life is but to deepen your awareness of your spiritual self, which is without question valuable and precious. Remind yourself that you are not striving to win literary awards with your efforts, you are merely telling your story in a forthright way. To feel reassured about the privacy of your writing, guard it with a password, if you are working on a computer, or find a secure place to keep your work in progress, where you can be certain no one will find it.

You may hit a low point in your productivity, not because of any worries that trouble you but merely because any long writing project tends to have peaks and valleys. If you have already filled half a notebook and your narrative has only reached adolescence, your heart may sink at the thought of all the pages still to be filled, all the story still to be told. Try taking a break, or jumping ahead in your story and writing about another part of your life entirely. You can fill in the intervening material later.

If you are temporarily at a loss for material, go to your memory log and read through it, selecting an event or episode and using that as a jumping-off point for a longer piece of writing that reveals something about your spiritual self. Decide later where this segment belongs in your life story.

You may fall silent when you come to a part of your autobiography that is painful or shameful. False starts may pile up, unsatisfactory drafts accumulate. You may feel like giving up. If so, be patient. You are probably not yet ready to relive the disturbing events. Decide to postpone writing that section and move to something more approachable.

Above all, move past your critical self by whatever means possible. For the task in hand you need encouragement, not criticism, approval, not censure.

TO SHARE—OR NOT TO SHARE

The issue of criticism naturally leads to a related question: should you share your spiritual autobiography with others? Earlier in this chapter the subject of privacy arose, and it is a crucial one. You are writing for yourself, after all; this is a very different act than writing for a public. Yet in the course of producing your work you may be tempted to ask a friend or relative to react to what you have written, either because you feel unsure or as a spur to further effort.

Be very careful whom you allow to read your work as it takes shape. An unsympathetic reader, or one who does not fully understand that you are telling the story of your spiritual life (or who may not understand what a spiritual life is), can dampen your enthusiasm by a thoughtless or inconsiderate response. A sympathetic reader, on the other hand, or someone who, because of their own life circumstances, can benefit from what you have written, can be trusted to give you heartening feedback.

The best readers are those who are engaged in the same effort you are, gathered together in a class or workshop in spiritual autobiography where a group leader can set up guidelines for nonjudgmental listening. In the workshop, each participant both reads from their own life story and listens to the writings of others. The sharing is powerful, and empowering.

Learning of the spiritual struggles, failures and triumphs of others makes us feel less alone in the midst of our own. It heightens our self-understanding and brings a helpful sense of proportion to the task of weaving together our own spiritual story.

Perhaps when you have completed your narrative you can consider whether or not to make it part of your legacy to those who survive you. We think with pleasure of passing down family heirlooms such as quilts or jewelry or antiques to future generations; why not pass down your account of the deepest part of yourself? A generation (or more) from now, your intimate revelations will be far less shocking or shameful than they may seem at the moment, but your honest narrative of your inner life will be, if anything, even more to be valued. Imagine how you would treasure a spiritual autobiography written by your grandparent or great-grandparent. No doubt it would be among your most prized possessions. Think of your work in this light, and consider leaving it to your heirs.

10

STANDING AT
THE CROSSROADS

$\mathcal{I}$n reading this book, and carrying out the exercises it invites you to do, you have gone on a journey of reflection.

You have stood outside your life and looked at it, as you would the life of a stranger, attempting to identify its shape and structure. You have analyzed your spiritual mentality, and identified important milestones, turning points and significant incidents in your past that go together to form the pattern of your days.

At the same time as you have stood outside your life, you have also entered it more deeply, going back in time, letting your memory carry you here and there throughout your past, pausing to reexperience former times and perhaps rescuing from oblivion long-buried recollections.

You have, by this time, done a good deal of writing. It is to be hoped that the writing is flowing smoothly; if not, it may help to return to Chapter 5 and review the techniques offered there.

For the past few days or weeks, however long it has taken you to work your way through these chapters, you have been focusing your attention on spiritual things. You have been spending time in the sphere of faith, "the sanctuary of life," in Paul Tillich's phrase, the holy of holies. Whether this has been an illuminating, expansive, or wrenching experience only you can say, but at least it lifted you, for a time, out of the realm of the ordinary and gave you a glimpse of the realm of the numinous.

As your process of reflecting deepened, you approached the threshold where finite and infinite conjoin, that threshold that is both within us and outside of us, and whose mystery all religious traditions seek to embrace.

In looking back over the course of your life you will have gained an appreciation for the waxing and waning of the spiritual impulse, how some seasons were rich in spiritual gifts and others were more meager. Our lives are full of inconsistencies, even contradictions; faith and doubt intertwine in complex ways, indeed, to an extent they evoke each other, though the hows and whys of that paradoxical linkage are the material of religious psychology, not spiritual autobiography.

At any rate, you will have gained greater respect

for the unpredictability and nuanced eccentricities of your spiritual life. Far from being a straight, unbroken, level path, the path of the spirit is often steep, twisting and strewn with thorns.

YOUR PATH AHEAD

The fact that you were drawn to undertake the writing of your spiritual story may indicate that you have come to a significant watershed in your inner life. Coming to terms with your past may seem a precondition to making a fresh start, beginning to trace a new and more purposeful path.

Possibly you have recently been more aware of your spiritual self and its longings, looking back across an abyss of unbelief or of spiritual deadness. Possibly you face an important decision, unsure of which choice to make; in that case arriving at a clearer sense of your spiritual history is helping to guide your choice. Possibly you have felt yourself moving toward the margins of faith, and want to explore the meaning of that shift in the context of your entire spiritual life. Whatever your present challenge, you have felt an urge to come to grips with your past, in order to gather strength through understanding.

You stand now at a crossroads.

Having acquired a clearer sense of the path along

which you have come, its form and shape, and with it a clearer sense of yourself as a spiritual wayfarer, you are in a position to choose your road ahead with greater discernment.

You know yourself better now. You are a pilgrim, with your eyes ever trained on the celestial city, seeking escape from the toilsome world with its allurements and snares. Or you are a seeker, on an eternal quest for understanding, touched by the grace of conversion. Or you are one burdened with adversity who has undergone a time of testing and is seeking healing and restoration. Or you are a prodigal son or daughter who, having wandered in the wilderness of your own lower nature, has set your feet on a homeward path. Or you have arrived at another definition of who you are, what your essential nature is and by what means you have thus far made your way through life.

Armed with this awareness, and cautioned about the pitfalls commonly experienced by one or another of these mentalities, you are prepared to forge ahead—but in which direction?

Pause now to consider your spiritual future. If you were to make a map of the journey that lies ahead for you, what destination would you choose for yourself? How would you know when you had arrived? What landmarks would lie along your route? Through what kingdoms or regions would you pass? What landscapes would you be careful to avoid?

In a sense, from now on you will be following this imaginary map, making these choices every day. Consciously or unconsciously, you will be charting a fresh spiritual course with each decision you make. It is to be hoped that, as you continue to compose your autobiography, while forging ahead with the business of more self-aware, purposeful living, your past and future will come into greater harmony in a rich and meaningful design.

My wish for you, dear reader, is that you will go on along paths of deeper discovery, never abandoning your quest, reaching out to find your best life. Take up your staff, plant your feet firmly in the way, and forge ahead!